IT'S THERE IN BLACK AND WHITE

It's There in BLACK and WHITE

✝

Scriptural Answers to 37 Questions People Are Asking about Racial Tension in the Church

GLENN COLLEY
BEN GISELBACH
HIRAM KEMP
MELVIN L. OTEY

© 2020 by Glenn Colley, Ben Giselbach, Hiram Kemp, Melvin L. Otey

All rights reserved. No part of this publication may be reproduced, stored in a retrieval system, or transmitted in any form or by any means without the prior written permission of the authors. The only exception is brief quotations in printed reviews.

ISBN-13: 978-0-9911139-5-8

Published by PlainSimpleFaith
http://www.plainsimplefaith.com

Printed in the United States of America

Unless otherwise noted, all Scripture quotations are from are from the New King James Version. Copyright © 1979, 1980, 1982 by Thomas Nelson, Inc. Used by permission. All rights reserved.

The Holy Bible, English Standard Version® (ESV®) Copyright © 2001 by Crossway, a publishing ministry of Good News Publishers. All rights reserved.

Cover Design: Ben Giselbach
Copy-editing: Tonja McRady

TABLE OF CONTENTS

AUTHORS' PREFACE 1

GLOSSARY OF KEY TERMS 3

Section 1
A LOOK AT OUR DIVERSE EXPERIENCES 5

Section 2
37 QUESTIONS PEOPLE ARE ASKING 12

   1. What is race? 13

   2. What is racism? 14

   3. Is racism just a "black" vs. "white" problem? 17

   4. What words of Jesus in the gospel accounts have a bearing on prejudice/racism today? 18

   5. At what point does a man or woman become more committed to his or her race than to Christianity? 20

   6. What distinguishes a racist Christian from one who is not? 22

   7. What is the difference between cultural preference and racism? 24

   8. How were racial problems handled in the first century church? Why should/shouldn't those solutions be our

pattern for today?	**26**
9. Is racism a problem in the church today?	**35**
10. Are church leaders commonly sweeping the history of racism under the rug today?	**37**
11. Weren't some of the great leaders of the Restoration Movement racist?	**38**
12. Are Christians guilty of being inconsistent in how we deal with racism?	**40**
13. Should Christians today repent and apologize for racial prejudices both past and present?	**41**
14. Where do we draw the line between cultural preference and scriptural authority?	**43**
15. Is it wrong for there to be a predominantly "white church" and "black church" in the same city?	**45**
16. How should Christians view "Critical Race Theory" in pursuing improved race relations?	**47**
17. What does the Bible say about slavery?	**49**
18. Is all slavery the same?	**51**
19. Is abortion, as promoted in the U.S. today, an example of racism?	**52**
20. Should Christians in the worship assembly celebrate leaders in the historical American Restoration Movement, MLK Jr. Day, Black History Month, or other national public figures?	**53**
21. Is it okay to sometimes speak in broad generalities about people groups?	**54**
22. To what extent can Christians be involved in social activism? In civil disobedience?	**55**

23. Can Christians be involved in protest? If so, what are the parameters involved? **58**

24. Is the matter of reparations biblical or purely social, and what does the Bible say about it? **59**

25. How should a Christian respond to religious groups that have racial supremacy built into their teachings?... **60**

26. When is it right for Christians to distance themselves from the values of their own ethnic culture?.................. **61**

27. What is systemic racism? What is white privilege? What role should these terms play in Christian discussions about race relations in the church? **63**

28. Does Scripture discourage interracial marriage? **64**

29. What role should race play in the selection of elders in a church today?.. **65**

30. How do I respond to the argument that Christianity is the "white-man's religion"? **66**

31. What is microaggression? How should it affect individuals in the church? **67**

32. How should I proceed if I hear someone in the church make a racially offensive comment? **72**

33. In what sense should Christians be "color-blind"? In what sense should they not?....................................... **74**

34. What role does/should anecdotal evidence play in discussions of racism? **76**

35. How can Christians discuss problems of racism without disrupting the unity of the church? What kinds of attitudes are counterproductive? **77**

36. What steps should congregations take in merging two culturally distinct congregations?.................................. **78**

37. What is the ultimate goal in discussions of racial divisions? **80**

Section 3
THE ROADMAP TO SOLVING RACIAL TENSIONS IN THE LOCAL CHURCH **83**

WORKS CITED **91**

SCRIPTURE INDEX **93**

*Behold, how good and how pleasant it is
for brethren to dwell together in unity!*
Psalm 133:1

AUTHORS' PREFACE

We hope this book will help Christians think about, discuss, and navigate sometimes challenging and sensitive questions regarding matters of race. We believe the Bible has the answers, and the church as designed by God—along with individual hearts obedient to Him—is the solution. We pray that this book will encourage and help us all as we endeavor to maintain the unity of the Spirit in the bond of peace.

In this way, the church should be an escape from the sorrow, anger, and strife propagated by the world. Christians may be ethnically diverse but they should be spiritually uniform. Congregations need to be places of serenity—a taste of paradise comprised of Christians who love, laugh, and assume the best about one another. Can this be found, even in today's climate? Yes! We've seen it with our own eyes. Peace is the power of the gospel (Romans 1:16; Ephesians 2:15)—a phenomenon people on the outside still find to be a mystery. But this warm, loving family atmosphere among the Lord's people is perhaps His greatest apologetic (John 13:34-35). Let the world see our love.

GLOSSARY OF KEY TERMS

Bias refers to prejudice in favor of or against one thing, person, or group, usually in a way that inhibits impartial judgment or that is considered to be unfair to another thing, person, or group.

Bigotry refers to strong partiality for a person's own group, religion, race, or politics and extreme intolerance for those who differ.

Discrimination, in the context of discussions about race, refers to acting on the preference for one class or category, or an aversion to a class or category, without due regard for individual merit.

Prejudice refers to preconceived opinions that are not necessarily based on reason or actual experience.

Racism (classical definition) refers to prejudice, discrimination, or antagonism directed against someone of a different race based on the belief that one's own race is superior.

Racism (Critical Race Theory definition) is a relatively recent adjustment to classical definition of racism, which requires a combination of two things: an attitude of prejudice and a position of power.

Color-blind, as it relates to race in sociology, is an ideal society where race is insignificant and does not limit an individual's opportunities. The word also describes those who attempt to treat everyone equally and not show favoritism or disdain based on race. Sometimes in the church, color-blind is just used to signify that someone sees humans as equally valuable (Galatians 3:27-28), but it may also indicate a failure to acknowledge the distinctive and admirable cultural qualities of black people.

Systemic racism, or institutional racism, refers to the policies of the dominant race or ethnicity found in institutions (e.g. criminal justice, healthcare, politics, employment, religion, housing) and the behavior of individuals who control these institutions and implement policies that are in some way designed to discriminate against a minority race or ethnic group.

White privilege is a shorthand way of referring to social advantage that a person automatically inherits simply by being "white," i.e., a Caucasian.

Microaggressions are small slights, whether intentional or unintentional.

Civil disobedience is loosely used to refer to a person's refusal to obey certain laws, demands, or orders by a governing body or representative in the name of a higher cause. More accurately understood, civil disobedience is the nonviolent or peaceful (that is, if this is truly "civil") refusal to obey certain laws, demands, or orders by a governing body or representative in the name of a higher cause.

A LOOK AT OUR DIVERSE EXPERIENCES

This book began as four gospel preachers, two black and two white, agreed to consider 37 of the most relevant questions about racial tensions that churches are currently facing. We then divided the questions among us and began individually writing the answers, emphasizing Scripture as our foundation for all answers. Then we painstakingly scrutinized one another's work until we could all live with the completed, finished responses. All four had the prerogative of walking away from the project at any time up until a contract was signed for publication. After all, broaching this volatile subject this way might be viewed as risky.

Writing this book together has been always loving, generally pleasant, sometimes arduous and challenging, yet always educational. As you read through our answers, you will pick up on the fact that we haven't always agreed; sometimes that shows in our answers. However, the issues over which we disagree pertained to the history of American slavery and various consequences that still linger in our present society. We have complete agreement on the fact that obeying Christ and teaching the truth of His New Testament is ultimately what will cure racism and bigotry. Our goal from the beginning was not to write a book in an effort to fix America's racial problems but rather to speak to the hearts of Christians about the church. *How can we keep the pain and destruction of racism out of the Lord's church?* It is our hope that this book can serve as a catalyst for improving and protecting unity with our brothers and sisters in Christ whose skin may be somewhat lighter or darker than ours.

We believe it will be of great benefit for you to begin this book by appreciating that our racial perspectives naturally stem from our unique life experiences in the church. With that in mind, we offer these short biographies:

Glenn Colley, a white man, was born in Houston, Texas, and grew up in a middle-class family with a mom and dad who loved one another and paid close attention to their children. Because his father was a preacher, they moved a few times and Glenn always attended a nearby public school. By his junior high years, schools were integrated, and Glenn had a circle of friends both black and white. He attended high school in Ardmore, Oklahoma, as part of a racially diverse student body. In the latter part of his high school education, he moved to Memphis where he attended Overton High School, a school in which white students were in the minority. His closest friends at this point were black.

He grew up being taught, even in a time when the world was reeling with racial division and while living in the town where Martin Luther King, Jr. was assassinated, that God made all people, and all deserve basic respect. Glenn was taught to live by a higher law than those written by men and that the mistreatment of anyone—even an enemy—was something Christians should always avoid.

Glenn has been preaching in churches of Christ for forty years and rejoices to see the large number of churches of Christ around the world in which Christians of different ethnicities are worshiping and working together in love.

Hiram Kemp, a black man, grew up in Hollywood, Florida, and became a Christian in 2009. Before becoming a Christian, however, he had several unfavorable interactions with law enforcement that certainly seemed discriminatory toward him as a minority. Growing up, he also witnessed what he would consider unfair treatment by law enforcement toward many of his family and friends.

Through the years, Hiram has had white, black, and Hispanic friends and was treated fairly by them all. He attended Bethune Cookman University, a HBCU (Historically Black College or University). Through the years, both Hiram and his wife have witnessed what they would consider white-on-black and black-on-white racism. Yet, since becoming a Christian in 2009, Hiram and his wife have spent considerable time around both black and white Christians and have seen the spirit of Christ displayed and practiced. They realize Christianity is the answer to racial tension. They have personally been treated very well by white and black people both inside and outside the church.

Ben Giselbach, a white man, was born in Indiana to a preacher's family. His family also moved several times, and most of the congregations in which he attended growing up were well integrated (a mixture of black, white, and some Hispanic). From childhood, many of his friends and church members whom he most admired were black. As far back as he can remember, his parents impressed upon him that character, not ethnicity, was what defined a person. In fact, in those intimate discussions between child and parent, Ben was taught that it didn't matter if he married a white or black girl, as long as she was a faithful Christian.

He has been blessed to not have seen very much firsthand of the ugliness racism brings. In the distant past during what was probably family reunion, Ben somewhat remembers overhearing a political discussion among non-Christian family members bemoaning how "the blacks are taking over." Years later, visiting a rural church, an elderly woman recommended the local high school because "only two or three black kids went to school there." But appalling comments like these so seldom entered Ben's ears that he can't remember many more like them. What Ben does have, however, are sweet memories of black and white Christians loving one another, worshiping together, and having one another in their homes. While Ben doesn't have much hope that the world will ever completely heal of its racism, he is a believer in the Lord's church and the power of the gospel to heal all wounds.

Melvin L. Otey, a black man, grew up in St. Louis, Missouri, lived in the District of Columbia for 17 years, and now resides in Montgomery, Alabama. He has attended "black schools" and "white schools" and worshipped at and preached with "black churches" and "white churches." He was exposed to racial bias and bigotry at a very early age and has witnessed and experienced it in personal, academic, professional, and religious settings throughout his life. In the course of his academic and personal studies, he has also invested considerable time studying the social and legal evolution of race relations in America. His personal conviction is that race relations have slowly and painstakingly improved, more or less in some instances, but that more must be done in order to reach the high standard that Jesus set, particularly for Christians.

RECOGNIZING THE RANGE OF INDIVIDUAL EXPERIENCES

To further illustrate that how diverse our life experiences are (and not merely in our skin color), we offer the experiences of the following people. Their real names have been withheld, but the four authors of this book can vouch for their credibility. The following accounts are not intended to be representatively proportionate of everyone in the church or the country. Rather, we simply want you to appreciate the vast range of experiences people have had.

Michelle is a black woman who—like Ben and Glenn—grew up in the church as a "preacher's kid." She attended Southwestern University (a HBCU) in Terrell, Texas. Her parents taught her and her siblings that they were not "African" but just American and—even more importantly—they were expected to find their primary identity in Christ. She never witnessed racism, or any of the consequences of racism (like discrimination or prejudice) happen in the church or among brethren. Outside the church, she did not experience any kind of prejudice from white people, yet she was never taught to look for it. If anything, she witnessed what she would consider "black-on-black" racism—

that is, prejudice among the black community based on physical features.

John, a white male, grew up in Montgomery, Alabama, in the middle of the Civil Rights Movement. Around the year 1970, when he was 15 years old, his father invited him to a church business meeting on the subject of integration. The meeting was prompted by a member who asked, "What if a black person wants to come to church here?" The meeting was heated, and terrible things were said. He remembers most vividly an 80-year-old woman who spoke up and said, "Why would we allow black people to come to church here when they don't even have souls?" At the time, the church had five elders. After the meeting, three of them voted for the congregation to remain segregated. John's father, the preacher, resigned after that decision.

Around that time, John transferred from public school to Alabama Christian School for the 9th grade. Alabama Christian, operated by Christians, was integrated well before schools were mandated to do so by the state. John's two closest friends were black twin brothers. One day, his dad dropped his friends and him off at the movie theatre. As they walked among the crowd by the ticket window, he remembers the hateful looks he received. One person shouted, "Look who they done brought to the movies!" (referring to John's black friends). Today, John says, "Thankfully, our country has changed a lot since then. […] Those were tense times. We have a long way to go, but compared to that era, there have been huge strides."

Marcus, a man who is half white and half black (his dad was black, his mom was white), grew up attending predominantly white congregations, mostly white schools, and lived in mostly white neighborhoods. He attended Faulkner University for a short while and also attended one of the brotherhood schools of preaching. He has never felt discriminated against or oppressed by white people based on his skin color. He has, however, been called racist names (such as "white-washed," "Oreo," "Uncle Tom," "house nigger") by black people simply because he was mixed and spent time among white people. Only once has he had an interaction with a law enforcement officer that "didn't feel right," but isn't sure whether it had anything to do with his ethnicity. Today he serves as a gospel preacher in a small town in the Deep South. Three years ago, he helped merge two congregations in his town—one predominately white, the other predominately black. While there were some small doctrinal disagreements the leadership had to navigate during the merger, Marcus can't remember any hint of racial tension.

Aaron, a white male, grew up Methodist but converted to Christianity when he was in high school. After college, he decided to become a youth minister and served at a small, entirely white congregation in East Alabama. One day, while going through a desk at the church building, he found a map of the community with sections crossed out. He asked one of the members what sections those were, and was told, "Those are where the blacks live. Stay out of those areas." A similar thing happened at his next work at a large congregation in Memphis, Tennessee, where he was told not to door knock in predominantly black neighborhoods. "We want to be a white, middle-class congregation," he was told. He was also told not to use any stock photos of black people on advertising material for the congregation "because we don't want to send the wrong message about who we are."

Kyle, a black man, is married to a white woman. Growing up, he remembers several girls who were forbidden to date him because he was black. In high school, the girl who would eventually become his wife invited him to church. She was the preacher's daughter. At the time he wasn't a Christian, but that visit led to Bible studies and eventually he was converted. Before he became a Christian, however, several families left the congregation because "the preacher's daughter was dating a black boy."

After getting married, Kyle graduated a brotherhood school of preaching and began looking for a congregation at which to preach. He feels very confident that several churches would not hire him because he was black, though it could also just be that he was an inexperienced preacher. After one particular "tryout," a member of one congregation said the elders would have hired them, "but they didn't like that he was black and she was white." From that point on, they learned to start sending a picture of their family along with their resume. It was clear—though never specifically stated—that they were not welcome at several congregations. As a whole, Kyle believes the church has been very good at overcoming prejudice and being shaped by the truth of the gospel. He and his wife have been welcomed and have been well received in many places.

SECTION 2

37 QUESTIONS PEOPLE ARE ASKING

1. WHAT IS RACE?

Modern scholarship is nearly unanimous that race has very little to do with biology or physical characteristics. C. Loring Brace, a biological anthropologist at the University of Michigan, says it succinctly: "Race is a social construct derived mainly from perceptions conditioned by events of recorded history, and it has no basic biological reality."[1]

We hold that there are not, technically speaking, multiple races. Every nation and people group trace their roots to one man—Adam. God "made from one man every nation of mankind to live on all the face of the earth, having determined allotted periods and the boundaries of their dwelling place" (Acts 17:26, ESV). The idea that there are different races is, ultimately, unbiblical. When we use the word *race* in this book, we are only using the word in an accommodative way. We are using it synonymously with the more accurate term of "people group." While there is such a thing as differing nationalities, ethnicities, cultures, there is technically no such thing as differing races. There is only one race—the human race.

When God designed the human body, He masterfully included a chemical in the skin called melanin—a pigment in the hair, skin, and irises. Biologists are still learning, but among other things, melanin seems to protect the body from the sun's ultraviolet rays. The longer you are exposed to the sun, the more melanin the human body tends to produce. Albino people are people whose bodies are unable to produce melanin. There is also another chemical called keratin—a protein that makes nails and hair hard and adds a yellow hue to human skin. A complicated set of genetic factors determine how much melanin and keratin the body will make. Thus, the color of one's skin is a combination of environment and genetics. Skin color is an immutable characteristic—people were born with their skin without any

---
[1] Robert Hotz, "Scientists Say Race Has No Biological Basis," *Los Angeles Times*, 20 February 1995

personal choice as to what color they wanted it to be. One's skin color is an immutable characteristic—they were born with their skin without any personal choice as to what color they wanted it to be.

The idea that a person's skin color is his or her primary identity is a core tenant of various hate groups such as the Ku Klux Klan and the Black Hebrew Israelites. We reject the idea that skin color plays any part in determining a person's worth. We affirm the fact that neither ethnicity nor melanin possesses intrinsic worth. These physical traits have no inherent desire, will, or conscience. They are incapable of hate or love nor can they discern between right and wrong. Such can only be influenced by the heart, not the skin.

For the Lord does not see as man sees; for man looks at the outward appearance, but the Lord looks at the heart. (1 Samuel 16:7)

2. WHAT IS RACISM?

Merriam-Webster offers the classical definition of racism, which is the belief "that race is the primary determinant of human traits and capacities and that racial differences produce an inherent superiority of a particular race." Racism is, therefore, a form of prejudice, which is "a stereotype accompanied by emotions that predispose a person to react in a consistent way (usually negative) toward a class of persons."[2]

A new definition of racism emerged in the 1970s and has increasingly been advocated. Joseph Barndt in his book *Dismantling Racism* succinctly defines racism as "prejudice plus power."[3] According to this new definition, a prejudiced person cannot be a racist unless he or she is in a position of social power or privilege. Thus, while a black person may be prejudiced,

---
2 David G. Benner and Peter C. Hill, eds., *Baker Encyclopedia of Psychology and Counseling*, n.pag.
3 Joseph R. Barndt, *Dismantling Racism: The Continuing Challenge to White America*, 28-29

only a white person can technically be racist simply because Caucasians represent a majority of the American population and Critical Race Theory (CRT) would designate white people as being in positions of power.

While we prefer the classical definition of racism over the new definition (we will only recognize the legitimacy of the classical definition throughout this book), we also understand that terminology changes over time. What we know, however, is that all forms of prejudice on the basis of ethnicity are sinful because the Bible condemns the sins of enmity. Racism, prejudice, and bigotry are sins that fall under the biblical umbrella word *enmity*, which is hostility, hatred, or antagonism towards another person.

Enmity (whether we are discussing racism or prejudice) is a great sin, not merely against another people group, but against God Himself. Laws, social policies, and attitudes which favor one race over another are a great evil and a blight to human dignity.

Racism is not merely a problem between blacks and whites, but it has plagued all peoples. There has been racism between Mexicans and blacks, Asians and whites, West Europeans and East Europeans, Chinese and Japanese, Indians and Arabs, etc., not to mention racism among Hispanic, African, and Asian subgroups. Consider the ethnic cleansing of Rwanda in 1994. Most people living in the United States of America would not be able to distinguish a Hutu from a Tutsi. Yet the Hutu extremists—believing their ethnicity was superior—murdered between 500,000 and 1,000,000 Tutsi Rwandans.

These examples of racism are products of man-made people categories. There was only one ethnic distinction made by God, and that was the distinct ethnic categorization of "Hebrew" and "Gentile." Yet, even *that* distinction has now been abolished by the coming of Christ (cf. Ephesians 2:11-22). Since Jews and Gentiles have been reconciled by God, then all people groups can be reconciled.

The bold message of Christianity is one of total equality in Christ. Part of

Christ's mission was to destroy the distinctions made by men, thus creating "one new man" (Ephesians 2:15). "For He Himself is our peace, who has made us both one and has broken down in His flesh the dividing wall of hostility," that He "might reconcile us both to God in one body through the cross, thereby killing the hostility" (vs. 14-16, ESV).

Wherever the concept of racism came from, it did not come from God. In reference to Gentiles, Peter (a Jew) said, "I understand that God shows no partiality, but in every nation anyone who fears Him and does what is right is acceptable to Him" (Acts 10:34-35, ESV). James taught, "My brothers, show no partiality as you hold the faith in our Lord Jesus Christ, the Lord of glory" (James 2:1, ESV). He then added, "If you show partiality, you are committing sin and are convicted by the law as transgressors" (vs. 9).

When Peter was guilty of discriminating against some people based upon ethnicity, Paul said, "I opposed him to his face, because he stood condemned" (Galatians 2:11). Later, in the same epistle, Paul revealed that "in Christ Jesus you are all sons of God, through faith. For as many of you as were baptized into Christ have put on Christ. There is neither Jew nor Greek, there is neither slave nor free, there is no male and female, for you are all one in Christ Jesus" (Galatians 3:26-28).

The message of the New Testament is consistent: All men are equal before God, all men are one in Christ, and all men have equal claim to the blood of Jesus and His kingdom. There is no room in Christianity for racism or ethnic prejudice.

One reason for this is because every human being is made in the image of God (Genesis 1:26-27). By virtue that every *Homo sapiens* has a soul, we all share the same Father (Numbers 16:22; 27:16; Job 12:10; Ecclesiastes 12:7; Isaiah 42:5; 57:16; Zechariah 12:1; Hebrews 12:9). Every human being, from a tiny embryo to a full-size adult, has equal value and infinite worth (cf. Matthew 16:26). We—regardless of our ethnicity, melanin level, physique, background, or age—have worth only because we are image-bearers of God.

There is a distinction to be made between ethnicity and culture, though these terms are often used interchangeably in popular vernacular. Culture includes beliefs, attitudes, and behavioral traits. Thus, we are biblically and morally bound to value some aspects of some cultures over others. Paul was not being racist when he quoted the popular observation, "Cretans are always liars, evil beasts, lazy gluttons" (Titus 1:12). He was observing that Cretan culture was saturated with sin—culturally, Cretans celebrated dishonesty, wickedness, laziness, and gluttony. Paul felt that many of the Christians in Crete, thankfully, had risen above their culture (cf. Titus 1:5-9).

There are aspects of every worldly culture, including our own (whichever culture is "ours"), that are sinful and thus in need of mortification. Christians are commanded to be discerning (Hebrews 5:14), and therefore we need to be able to commend what is good about any given culture while also be able to criticize whatever is evil about a given culture. The kingdom of Christ should not celebrate a diversity of worldly cultures so much as it should transcend worldly cultures.

3. IS RACISM JUST A "BLACK" VS. "WHITE" PROBLEM?

Racism is not merely a "black" and "white" problem. America has its own unique history of problems with racism that includes codifying, normalizing, and enforcing hatred and oppression based on skin color. However, the system of apartheid in South Africa, Hitler's campaign of extermination against European Jews, and the Rwandan genocide are obvious and prominent examples illustrating that the sin of racial hate and oppression is pervasive throughout the world and is not limited to America's painful and sometimes tortured history of problems between "whites" and "blacks."

Even if one confines his consideration to the American context of racism, though, the problem is broader than we sometimes think. Racism is not merely a problem between the races or ethnic groups; it is a problem within individual hearts. Harboring racist ideologies is sinful because it violates Jesus' command to love one's neighbors (Luke 10:25-37) and harms the individual who harbors them even if, for the sake of argument, the ideologies are never acted upon (consider Mark 7:20-23). In this regard, any person, regardless of skin color or nationality, can be a racist.

4. WHAT WORDS OF JESUS IN THE GOSPEL ACCOUNTS HAVE A BEARING ON PREJUDICE/RACISM TODAY?

In speaking primarily to first century Jews throughout His earthly ministry, Jesus did not have occasion to address problems of interracial or intercultural prejudices in ways that might immediately resonate with twenty-first century Americans. The most prominent cultural prejudices of His day centered on the relationship between the Jews and their Samaritan neighbors. The Samaritans were a people of mixed heritage, the result of intermarrying between the remnant of the Northern Kingdom of Israel and foreign colonists imported by the conquering Assyrians. Their religious doctrine and practice was a mixture of both pagan and Mosaic traditions (2 Kings 17:24-41).

There was significant and lasting animosity between the Samaritans and their neighbors in Judah. For example, when the Jews returned from Babylonian captivity, they refused Samaritan assistance in reconstructing the temple, and the Samaritans subsequently tried to undermine their efforts (Ezra 4). The hatred between them became even more intense during the Intertestamental period of the Maccabees when Hasmonean King John Hyrcanus marched against Samaria and destroyed the temple on Mount Gerazim. In Jesus' day, it was well settled that the Jews had "no dealings with the Samaritans" (John 4:9).

Jesus confronted long-standing Jewish prejudices against the Samaritans. First, He was intentional about going into Samaria and interacting with the people there (e.g., Luke 9:52; John 4:4). He even initiated a public conversation with a Samaritan woman, which surprised both her (John 4:9) and His disciples (John 4:27). In the course of their talk, Jesus helped the woman spiritually by addressing her sins and talking with her about salvation, and He was subsequently able to reach others through her. Jesus referred to this activity as doing the will of God and accomplishing His work (John 4:33-34). The Samaritans, whom the Jews held in disdain, were part of the spiritual harvest God expected to reap (John 4:35). Despite the deep and abiding animosities between the two peoples, Jesus remained in that city for two days teaching the people and allowing them to know Him as the Savior of the world (John 4:39-42).

On another occasion, Jesus presented an anonymous Samaritan as epitomizing the Old Testament command to love one's neighbor as he loved himself (Luke 10:29-37). When a man fell prey to thieves on the treacherous road from Jerusalem down to Jericho, Jewish religious leaders saw him but failed to render aid, even though they were, presumably, of the same nationality (vs. 30-32). In what would have been a surprise for Jesus' Jewish listeners, a Samaritan happened along and, being moved with compassion (vs. 33), treated the fallen stranger's wounds, put the man on his animal, transported him to an inn, and cared for him overnight. The next day before the Samaritan departed, he paid for the injured man's continued care (vs. 33-35). He did all of this without any apparent expectation of recompense or accolade for a man who might well have immediately despised him because of his heritage. The Samaritan demonstrated the truth declared throughout the Bible that God does not show favor or partiality based on things like genealogy or culture (Acts 10:34-35; Romans 2:11; Ephesians 6:9; 1 Peter 1:17), and that godly people must not do so either in loving their neighbors (e.g., Proverbs 24:23; James 2:1), even if there are cultural differences and historical animosities. He treated the fallen stranger as he would have wanted to be treated had he been in the stranger's place (Matthew 7:12).

Just before His ascension, Jesus commanded the Apostles to continue bearing witness of Him in the world—including Samaria (Acts 1:8)—and despite the cultural differences that persisted between Jews and Samaritans, Christians preached the gospel in Samaria and converted many (Acts 8:12-13). This was a direct consequence of their following Jesus' example and teaching. Jesus expected His disciples to rise above and overcome their various prejudices in order to love their neighbors as they loved themselves. He showed them by His actions, and He taught them in His doctrine.

5. AT WHAT POINT DOES A MAN OR WOMAN BECOME MORE COMMITTED TO HIS OR HER RACE THAN TO CHRISTIANITY?

Have we turned our race or our culture into an idol? Here are a few questions to ask ourselves:

- Do I feel someone should go to another congregation based on upon the predominance of a certain people group?
- Am I satisfied with being a Christian? Or do I need to further label myself as a "black," "white," or "Latino" Christian?

- Do I find myself more passionate about my views on race relations than I am the gospel? Am I more outspoken about racism than I am about other sins?

- Am I willing to divide the church over this if brethren don't see things exactly as I do?

- Am I willing to endorse or otherwise align myself with false teachers or other forces of wickedness for what I perceive as the higher cause of my social platform?

Christianity is fundamentally a religion that necessitates dying to self (Luke 9:23). Pride is too heavy a burden to carry in addition to our cross. If I have more pride in my racial ethnicity or more passion for my earthly heritage, or even if I hold these things as being of equal weight with my relationship with the Lord, then I am guilty of idolatry. Why are some Christians so sensitive about our ethnicity or culture? Perhaps it is because we think too highly of ourselves to begin with (cf. 1 Corinthians 4:7).

Blood may be thicker than water, but truth is thicker than blood. Jesus says, "Whoever does the will of My Father in heaven is My brother and sister and mother" (Matthew 12:50). In other words, Jesus says, "You want to know who My people are? Those who obey God." Christians are part of a bigger family—a family that dwarfs genetics. "Your people" are not primarily those who share your ethnicity ("broad is the way that leads to destruction" includes people who share your ethnicity, cf. Matthew 7:13-14). "Your people" are Christians.

6. WHAT DISTINGUISHES A RACIST CHRISTIAN FROM ONE WHO IS NOT?

What sets apart a Christian who is racist isn't merely that someone has called him a racist. The glossary of terms offered in this book defines *racist* this way: "A racist is one who believes that race accounts for differences in human character or ability and that a particular race is superior to others."

We think all readers agree that racism is sinful. Because all races are created by God (Acts 17:26) and because the Bible says Christians from all nations (Revelation 7:9) will be in heaven, no race should be viewed as superior. Perhaps we'd do well, as with all spiritual matters, to try our best to use Bible terms. Instead of using the word *racism* that is admittedly used to describe a variety of attitudes and behaviors, for our purposes here let's use the scriptural term *enmity*. Enmity is "a feeling or condition of hostility; hatred; ill will; animosity; antagonism." To have enmity toward another, especially a fellow Christian, is sin (1 John 3:15).

Consider how the word *enmity* is used in the following verses:

> *That very day Pilate and Herod became friends with each other, for previously they had been at **enmity** with each other."* (Luke 23:12) (Strong's defines the Greek word *echthra/enmity* as "hostility; by implication, a reason for opposition").

> *Because the carnal mind is **enmity** against God; for it is not subject to the law of God, nor indeed can be."* (Romans 8:7)

> *Adulterers and adulteresses! Do you not know that friendship with the world is **enmity** with God? Whoever therefore wants to be a friend of the world makes himself an enemy of God."* (James 4:4)

The word *enmity* is not inherently about race; it is about harboring animosity or hatred and is a sinful attitude in one man toward another (or toward God). What I believe most people mean when they accuse a man of being a racist is that he has enmity in his heart toward people of another race.

This question seems so simple. No *faithful* Christians are racists. You can know this by the way they treat those of another race. They speak warmly to and about all people. They befriend people regardless of color. It is their nature to avoid hurtful behavior and language. They evangelize people without regard to color and see all souls of equal value to the Almighty. It really should be simple and obvious.

Some brethren believe they predominantly see racial tension, bigotry, and prejudice in the church. They believe that the culture in America—the very soul of American society—is racist and always has been. As the argument goes, because people converted to Christianity are the products of that culture when they enter the church, then the church is permeated with racism. As one brother put it, "You start getting taught in America before you can make a decision. You start getting indoctrinated before you can put up a fight of resistance. By the time you are old enough to make decisions, you can only make decisions from what's in your head… you are so impacted and converted (for lack of a better word), it's put into your head space. It is a system and indoctrination into beliefs that you have to unlearn when you meet Jesus."

The apostle Paul goes to great lengths to describe the church of Christ in the image of a human body with feet, hands, and eyes—illustrating the fact that we are all different, and yet together we make up one body in Christ (1 Corinthians 12:12-27). In this Christian economy, even our members considered weak by the world are highly valued (1 Corinthians 12:23-25). Christians value people primarily because of who created them (Acts 17:26-29), and then because of who saved them when they were baptized (Galatians 3:27-29). In Christ we—black or white or any other color—make up the "one another" references in the New Testament (e.g., Galatians 6:2).

Racism is sinful, but it does not permeate the church today. We could say the same thing about other sins such as adultery. There is no question that racial tension exists in some congregations of the church, but she is not permeated with it. We must be careful to think the best of one another. Not every insensitive comment grows out of a racist heart, and not every concern raised about prejudice or bigotry is an effort to cause division. If such mindsets are brought into the church, confusion and division will result. Sometimes today sincere Christians, who are not racists according to our working definition of the term, are strongly resisted when they offer evidence that they are, in fact, *not* racists.

What we preach about enmity must be preached equally to all. True unity in congregations of the church of Christ will not fully exist unless Christians of all races can be viewed with love, and that includes the presumption of innocence until the evidence truly proves otherwise. We cannot simply let the worldly and evolving rules about microaggression be our standard. Our standard must be the New Testament pattern, equal for all, in love and in view of living in eternity together in the land that is "incorruptible, undefiled, and that never fades away" (1 Peter 1:3-4).

A person who believes a particular race is inherently superior to another is a racist and shows enmity in his heart whatever his color. Sometimes selfishness in the form of bigotry or prejudice creeps into our hearts. Let us go out of our way to make our brethren of differing ethnicities and cultures comfortable around us.

7. WHAT IS THE DIFFERENCE BETWEEN CULTURAL PREFERENCE AND RACISM?

Every individual is socialized in the norms of some culture. The word *culture* refers to a mostly intangible web of various aspects of group life, including customs, traditions, values, behaviors, beliefs, languages, and social forms. These things are shared among members of a particular group, passed along from generation to generation, and distinguish their way of life from others. Cultural differences are inevitable because groups of people live in different environs, have different resources, have different experiences, and so forth. Moreover, a person naturally would be more familiar and comfortable with the norms of his or her own culture, including things like its cuisine, rituals, and social expectations.

The Bible does not offer an examination of distinct cultures, but the existence of varying ways of life between various people groups is evident throughout (e.g., Genesis 50:1-3; Ruth 4:7; Daniel 6:8; John 2:6; Acts 16:19-21; 1 Corinthians 11:4-16). For example, Jacob was surprised when he was given the older of two sisters in marriage in part because he was unfamiliar with the marital expectations and norms of the people in Paddan-aram (Genesis 29:21-26). In the New Testament, Porcius Festus acknowledged that, among the Romans, men were not to be condemned without first being given the opportunity to face their accusers and defend against the relevant charges (Acts 25:13-16). Not every culture shared this expectation regarding the administration of justice. Moreover, Festus confessed that he was not familiar enough with Jewish custom to confidently judge the matters being disputed (Acts 25:17-20). Later, in speaking to Agrippa, the apostle Paul averred that the king, unlike Festus, was learned in the various "customs and questions" that existed among the Jews (Acts 26:1-3).

Even in Christ where the bonds that unify Christians should be stronger than any cultural preference, there is nothing inherently wrong with acknowledging cultural differences and having greater affinity for various aspects of one culture over another. Racism, however, is obviously a wholly different matter. As we typically define *racism* in the context of American culture, the idea has more to do with skin complexion or ethnicity than it does with culture. Racism involves a belief in the superiority of one race over another along with the attendant prejudices and discriminations that flow from that belief. This is not a proper or necessary consequence of having certain cultural preferences. Paul seems to have rather easily associated with people of various cultures in his ministry (1 Corinthians 9:20-22; Acts 17:17-28) while resisting improper attempts to bind spiritually irrelevant aspects of one culture on members of other cultures (Galatians 2:3-5). We can investigate, appreciate, and celebrate cultures and acknowledge the differences without denigrating or demonizing them. This readily distinguishes preferences from bigotry and racism.

8. HOW WERE RACIAL PROBLEMS HANDLED IN THE FIRST CENTURY CHURCH? WHY SHOULD/SHOULDN'T THOSE SOLUTIONS BE OUR PATTERN FOR TODAY?

The Christian's compass and final authority is the Bible. Again, the Word completely furnishes us to every good work (2 Timothy 3:16-17). It answers every false doctrine and lights our path for dealing with any struggle (Psalm 119:105). It must be all of that for Christians in reference to the subject of this book.

There has never been a day in the church's existence void of cultural differences. The day the church was birthed boasted of Jews and proselytes from over a dozen diverse places. Acts 2:9-11 records:

> Parthians and Medes and Elamites, those dwelling in Mesopotamia, Judea and Cappadocia, Pontus and Asia, Phrygia and Pamphylia, Egypt and the parts of Libya adjoining Cyrene, visitors from Rome, both Jews and proselytes, Cretans and Arabs—we hear them speaking in

our own tongues the wonderful works of God.

We read in Scripture many times of nationalities/cultures being brought together in the church and we often see how they resolved problems between them.

Regardless of color, in the church we share a dedication to our King Jesus and a commitment to restoring New Testament Christianity. Let's take a look at racial distinctions in the first century and how issues were handled when people of different races came together in the church.

GALATIANS 3:26-29

> For you are all sons of God through faith in Christ Jesus. For as many of you as were baptized into Christ have put on Christ. There is neither Jew nor Greek, there is neither slave nor free, there is neither male nor female; for you are all one in Christ Jesus. And if you are Christ's, then you are Abraham's seed, and heirs according to the promise.

Imagine the weight of these words in that first century culture: "There is neither Jew nor Greek…" or "…there is neither slave nor free." Clear and dramatic distinctions in those people existed in their culture, sometimes perhaps enough that they could have felt justified in hating each other. God's answer to the differences was unity in Christ: "You are all one in Christ Jesus." How would this read if it were written today in America with our racial issues being considered? We cannot imagine it excluding words such as, "There is neither white nor black nor brown; you are all one in Christ Jesus." This passage is as close to our current problems as we can imagine, and it teaches that the resolution is unity and a disregard for skin color in the church. We are *one in Christ*.

The New Testament's method for the spiritual kingdom to correct and avoid racial tension has never been church upheaval. The answer has always been that there is one body in Christ—a body in which every person is loved regardless of, and independently of, nationality or ethnicity. Unity, regardless of color, is the biblical goal. The passage does not mean that there really were no native Jews or native Greeks. Of course there were. It did not mean that there were literally no slaves or free men. There were. It does not mean that there were no genders. Of course people could tell the difference between men and women. But the Scripture means there were no distinctions in value. To be blind to distinctions that would cause us to value one person's fellowship more than another is a scriptural goal.

Some are concerned that if we follow the apostle Paul's teaching of "neither Jew nor Greek" we will fail to recognize the distinctive and special gifts that various people bring to the table. That view is eclipsed by truth in Christ: None of us bring any gift worthy of even being at the table when it is the feast of the Lamb. It is only His blood that makes us worthy. His blood makes us all worthy to the same exact degree.

In the infant church we see an instance when Christians brought unique ethnic qualities to benefit the church. Read on:

ACTS 6:1-7

> Now in those days, when the number of the disciples was multiplying, there arose a complaint against the Hebrews by the Hellenists, because their widows were neglected in the daily distribution. Then the twelve summoned the multitude of the disciples and said, "It is not desirable that we should leave the word of God and serve tables. Therefore, brethren, seek out from among you seven men of good reputation, full of the Holy Spirit and wisdom, whom we may appoint over this business; but we will give ourselves continually to prayer and to the ministry of the word." And the saying pleased the whole multitude. And they chose Stephen, a man full of faith and the Holy Spirit, and Philip, Prochorus, Nicanor, Timon, Parmenas, and

Nicolas, a proselyte from Antioch, whom they set before the apostles; and when they had prayed, they laid hands on them. Then the word of God spread, and the number of the disciples multiplied greatly in Jerusalem, and a great many of the priests were obedient to the faith.

The Hellenistic (or Grecian) Jews are first mentioned in the Bible in this passage. The Christians on this occasion were divided into two groups. The first were those who had remained in Judea near Jerusalem, used the Hebrew language, and who were appropriately called "Hebrews." The second group consisted of those who were scattered among the Gentiles, who spoke the Greek language and used the Greek translation of the Old Testament called the Septuagint. These were called "Hellenists," from a word meaning "Greek" or "Greek-speaking." To "Hellenize" is to adopt Greek culture and ideas.

Dissensions arose between the Hellenistic Jews and the Hebraic Jews. Apparently, the Hellenistic Jews from other parts of the world were made to feel like outsiders. Sadly, the strife between the two groups was not automatically eliminated by their conversion to Christianity, as illustrated by the complaints concerning food distribution to widows of the two groups. The church of the first century was not immune to issues (or tensions) of race and/or culture. Whether the neglect of these particular widows was intentional is not stated, but we assume so, because the Hellenists issued a complaint not merely an observation.

The Apostles quickly called an assembly of the church and explained that, while it was not possible for them to leave their work to serve tables, they would address the obvious conflict between these two groups. Their judgment was this: "Therefore, brethren, seek out from among you seven men of good reputation, full of the Holy Spirit and wisdom, whom we may appoint over this business" (vs. 3). Notice that they didn't just call a meeting of the Jewish Christians or the Hellenist Christians: "Then the twelve summoned the multitude of the disciples" (vs. 2). The decision was to select men whom they judged to be devout, respected, and righteous Christians to take care of this obvious inequity. Everyone agreed that this was a good remedy for the problem: "And the saying pleased the whole multitude" (vs. 5). Seven men were selected: "Stephen, a man full of faith and the Holy Spirit, and Philip, Prochorus, Nicanor, Timon, Parmenas, and Nicolas, a proselyte from Antioch, whom they set before the apostles; and when they had prayed, they laid hands on them" (vs. 5). The problem was solved: "Then the word of God spread, and the number of the disciples multiplied greatly in Jerusalem, and a great many of the priests were obedient to the faith" (vs. 7).

Now, let's draw some observations:

1. The men whom the church selected were Greeks/Hellenists. We see this from their Grecian names. The Apostles apparently didn't dictate that the men be Grecians; instead, they submitted to the "…neither Jew nor Greek" principle and race did not matter. They simply insisted that the men selected were righteous and respected by the faithful Christians. The church decided to select Greek men. It isn't necessarily wrong to consider a man's race or cultural background when choosing him for a particular work in the church. Sometimes his race makes him better suited for a task. In this case it was reasonable for the church to select Grecians. These men would be sensitive to the needs of these widows. Choosing these seven men not only fixed the problem of the daily ministration, but it also eliminated the potential of a racial issue being raised in the future in regard to the widows.

2. The problem that created this racial tension was a practical one and easily identifiable. When people of the world see a problem that relates to race, they may merely want to start a dialogue that, by its nature, never ends, and identify a problem that is designed to *never be solved.* This was not so in the church. The Apostles simply saw the problem of the church dividing over this inequity and they fixed it. All the widows should be cared for, regardless of race. Period.

3. The remedy had one practical result in mind: equality. Equal access to the blessings of fellowship. The Christian widows of Grecian heritage and the widows of Jewish heritage were to be treated the same.

Again, a key factor in solutions to church problems is this pattern: The sin was objectively identified, then correction was made. Note that after the church chose men of the same culture/nationality to handle the problem, it was considered by the church to be fixed (so far as scriptural history goes). The church went back to converting the lost to Christ.

ROMANS 15:25-27

> But now I am going to Jerusalem to minister to the saints. For it pleased those from Macedonia and Achaia to make a certain contribution for the poor among the saints who are in Jerusalem. It pleased them indeed, and they are their debtors. For if the Gentiles have been partakers of their spiritual things, their duty is also to minister to them in material things.

Here is a remarkable example of Gentile Christians helping Jewish Christians. The Jewish Christians hadn't always been kind to them; yet Christ taught unity and sacrifice. They sent aid. Imagine the effect this must have had on the poor Jewish Christians of Judea. Paul taught in Romans 12:20 principles about how we should deal with our enemies. While the Gentile Christians may not have viewed the Jews as their enemies on this occasion, they practiced the command: "If your enemy is hungry, feed him; if he is thirsty, give him a drink; for in so doing you will heap coals of fire on his head." It is difficult to hate a man who is willing to help when you are down. That's what the Gentiles did for their Jewish brothers in Christ.

Christians today must not look at the church with the world's answers to racial problems, but instead through the eyes of New Testament revelation. Souls do not come in colors, and all souls equally matter. We are compelled by Christ to warmly help fellow Christians when they are hurting.

What we are saying would not garner the approval of some worldly leaders right now but does have the approval of the King of Kings. It has the approval of our Master, whether you are black or white, Hispanic or Asian.

ACTS 10:28

> Then he said to them, "You know how unlawful it is for a Jewish man to keep company with or go to one of another nation. But God has shown me that I should not call any man common or unclean."

Remember that Peter had been sent by the Lord to a Gentile's house—that of Cornelius. Peter made it clear that a great change had been made between the Old Law and the New, in order that the sacrifice of Christ would be made equally available to all nations of people.

There were times in the American church when the sinful racism of the world elbowed its way into the church and produced wickedness in some Christians; but as in Acts 10, sincere Christians have adopted the will of their Lord and, when in error, have changed.

The difference between what Peter was describing and our circumstance today is that he was exiting adherence to a law of God that had been fulfilled and nailed to the cross (Colossians 2:14), while we have exited an American (racist and forced) slavery of men—a situation which was always wrong, unlike the adherence to the Old Law. Happily, we have seen a positive transformation in American congregations of the churches of Christ. It has not been a perfect transformation because people are imperfect, but faithful Christians are not racists, and there are many faithful congregations of Christians today.

GALATIANS 2:6-7, 11-15

> But from those who seemed to be something—whatever they were, it makes no difference to me; God shows personal favoritism to no man—for those who seemed to

> be something added nothing to me. But on the contrary, when they saw that the gospel for the uncircumcised had been committed to me, as the gospel for the circumcised was to Peter....(vs. 6-7)
>
> Now when Peter had come to Antioch, I withstood him to his face, because he was to be blamed; for before certain men came from James, he would eat with the Gentiles; but when they came, he withdrew and separated himself, fearing those who were of the circumcision. And the rest of the Jews also played the hypocrite with him, so that even Barnabas was carried away with their hypocrisy. But when I saw that they were not straightforward about the truth of the gospel, I said to Peter before them all, "If you, being a Jew, live in the manner of Gentiles and not as the Jews, why do you compel Gentiles to live as Jews?" (vs. 11-15)

Peter knew that Jesus brought equality for all men in the church, but not all Christians were behaving as if they understood this. At church potlucks, Peter was eating with the Gentile Christians; perhaps even eating food (such as pork) that would have previously been unclean to the Jews. But when Jewish Christians entered, who were wrong to oppose mixing races this way, Peter moved to a different table. Paul saw him and knew exactly what Peter was doing. We all agree that Paul did the right thing to challenge his fellow apostle Peter. It is right for the leaders in our congregations to strongly correct this sort of problem when it rears its head. Yet, observe that Peter's moving to a different table was not a small slight. It was bad behavior and was inconsistent with discipleship. It was thus corrected in clear terms. This is still right today.

If a white or black Christian brother similarly did today what Peter did back then, good elders and others would correct him—not because he violated any of the ever-changing virtues of secular society, but because he had violated God's will. God is no respecter of persons, and because we are

God's priests (1 Peter 2:9), we cannot communicate anything different. We cannot excuse this kind of behavior today by saying, "He's from a different era." Incidentally, that's what Peter was—a man from a different era. Yet, now that Peter was a citizen of the kingdom of Christ, he should have understood that ethnic bigotry is always wrong. What if a member today persists in the bigoted behavior for which Peter was rebuked? Romans 16:17 instructs us that after our efforts to restore him, he (or she) should be marked and avoided, for he (or she) is creating obstacles in the unity of the church.

PHILEMON

This is an amazing chapter in Scripture. It is a letter to a master carried by a runaway slave who had become a Christian while a fugitive. The slave Onesimus was being sent back by Paul the apostle (vs. 12) to set matters straight with the Christian slave owner Philemon. Among other things Paul wrote this:

> For perhaps he departed for a while for this purpose, that you might receive him forever, no longer as a slave but more than a slave—a beloved brother, especially to me but how much more to you, both in the flesh and in the Lord. (Philemon 1:15-16)

It was clear to Paul that Onesimus would be glad to be brothers with Philemon and Philemon should feel the same. We are not told how it turned out but are left to assume that the weight of Paul's influence on them both accomplished its purpose.

It is significant that Paul did not demand that Philemon free Onesimus from his position as a slave. Perhaps that's because the Scriptures do not promote disobeying civil law (Romans 13:1-7), except in cases where civil law requires us to sin. Paul demanded only that they love and respect one another. What they decided about the slavery was left to their consciences upon recognizing that they were brethren. We naturally assume that

Philemon made Onesimus' life much better.

This isn't the only time slavery is mentioned as existing among Christians in the first century. We want you to consider that Paul didn't posit that those slaves, as a segment of the church, should now receive unique treatment. Rather, they were to be honored by the highest treatment—that offered by the Golden Rule, which of course excluded any mistreatment. The highest privilege for all was the same: the joy of being forgiven and fully included (enjoying fellowship) by and with a group of forgiven people anticipating heaven (Matthew 5:11-12).

One major implication we see in the book of Philemon, along with *every other passage* discussing brother love and treatment, is this: How could a slave owner, who is a Christian for long, continue to have a heart for treating a fellow image-bearer as a piece of property?

9. IS RACISM A PROBLEM IN THE CHURCH TODAY?

If we distinguish between prejudice, bias, bigotry, and racism rather than lumping these concepts together, it seems unlikely that racism is a pervasive problem in the church today. For better or for worse, though, people in America are reared and socialized in its culture and bring some of that culture into the church when they are converted. To the extent and degree that even some Christians harbor ethnic animus—and some do—it is fair to say that racial prejudice and bigotry is a problem in the church.

Problems of this kind are as old as the church itself, and this is evident in the New Testament. For example, in Galatians 2, Paul demonstrates that bigotry was an issue among Christians in the first century. Either the apostle Peter's own bigotry against non-Jews resurfaces or he yields to the bigoted influence of some of his peers when he withdraws himself from Gentile Christians at Antioch (Galatians 2:11-14). In America, most congregations typically followed suit with the larger society for many years, upholding and enforcing bigoted and racist social customs that reinforced the idea that persons of African descent were inferior and, in decades gone by, some Christians were open and adamant in their insistence on maintaining these norms. Christian assemblies and Christians schools generally remained segregated even after state laws that required it were abolished.

Because ethnic prejudice, bigotry, and racism are still issues in America, there are still issues, more or less, in the church in America. Racial animus has lessened and is more subtle today than in former times, both in society at large and in the church. While we do not have mandated segregation today, the simple truth is that the Sunday morning worship hour is still one of the most, if not the most, segregated hour of any given week. Moreover, there are occasions where visitors to a congregation are told, or at least it is clearly intimated, that they would probably be more comfortable at a church "down the road" or "across town" where the members look more like the visitors. Also, we still have separate schools, lectureships, campaigns, and such like. These are vestiges of former times when social segregation based on racial hate was compelled and enforced by law and custom.

In short, yes—racial biases and bigotry are still problems in the church today. Thankfully, the problems are not as extreme as they were in former times, but more progress can and must be made.

10. ARE CHURCH LEADERS COMMONLY SWEEPING THE HISTORY OF RACISM UNDER THE RUG TODAY?

It is impossible to know what every church leader in every place is doing or what each leader believes. Still, here are some things each church leader must consider regarding the subject of racism. The issue of race must be addressed from our pulpits and in our Bible classes because it is a Bible subject. When Peter practiced prejudice, Paul withstood him to his face because he was not walking upright according to the gospel (Galatians 2:11-14). Those practicing racism are out of step with the gospel and must be corrected. However, though racism is commented on and condemned in Scripture, church leaders must be sure that it does not become the main topic in our churches or the only matter discussed. To the degree that any issue or topic is emphasized more than Jesus Christ, churches become imbalanced and unsound (cf. 1 Corinthians 2:1-2). Church leaders must ensure that the "whole counsel of God" is proclaimed and this includes discussions on racism (Acts 20:26-27). Nevertheless, the problem of racism is not solved by emphasizing racism continually but instead by preaching the gospel and calling all men and women to unify under the cross of Jesus. While church leaders should emphasize some troubles because they are prevalent in society or highlighted by current events, these matters should not be allowed to "drive" congregations. Otherwise, even if they are popular with some contemporaries, they will become biblically unbalanced.

11. WEREN'T SOME OF THE GREAT LEADERS OF THE RESTORATION MOVEMENT RACIST?

No doubt, some were. We wish we could say that all members of the Lord's church have always risen above culture in which they were born by living free of all prejudice. Sadly, that has not always been the case. In the first century, the apostle Peter and Barnabas were men of their day and allowed themselves to get caught up in the Jewish prejudice against the Gentiles (Galatians 2:11-14). Occasionally, people point to instances of racial prejudice among our own people of yesteryear. The most glaring example we know of is the infamous 1941 article by Foy E. Wallace Jr. in the *Bible Banner* entitled "Negro Meetings for White People."[4] In it he bemoans reports of white women going up to black preachers and "holding their hands in both of theirs" after their lively preaching. Wallace believed that it was improper for a woman to "lower herself" to the level of holding a black man's hand. Wallace then gave an example of what he thought was more becoming of a white man. He recalled a moment following a gospel meeting when N.B. Hardeman refused to shake the hands of some "negroes," offering instead to talk to them privately outside. Wallace adds, "I think he was right." We could procure a few other examples, but that is not our purpose. Before moving on, we feel there are a few observations that must be made.

First, there is no excuse for prejudice. Racism, like many other sinful behaviors, is often conditioned in a person's formative years. Such temptations are based on feelings and perceptions—feelings and perceptions that are flawed. Christians are never commanded to live as they feel. It is a cross we are called to bear and not give in to. Regardless of upbringing, we still bear the responsibility to find the truth and sell it not (Proverbs 23:23).

Second, we feel it is of utmost importance to remind ourselves that any

---

[4] Foy E. Wallace, "Negro Meetings for White People," *Bible Banner* (March 1941), 7

allegation of racism is just that—an allegation. If there is credible evidence, we should call sin "sin." Yet, we should be slow to believe allegations of prejudice, as we will be judged with the same standard of judgment we place on others (Matthew 6:12, 14-15). Furthermore, how shall we practice the Golden Rule in this matter (Matthew 7:12)? *We all hope the next generation will be charitable in its judgments about us.* Genuine love "thinks no evil" (1 Corinthians 13:6). Instead, love "believes all things, hopes all things" (1 Corinthians 13:7).

Third, we must not forget the instances of *commendable* behavior of our brethren in times of racial angst. In the mid-1900s, the West Huntsville church of Christ was hosting a tent meeting in a predominantly black community, and Marshall Keeble was the visiting preacher. The minister at West Huntsville John Jenkins invited Keeble to his house for supper. Upon arrival, Keeble refused to enter the house, saying to him that his neighbors "would be mean to you and burn a cross in your yard." So Jenkins told his two sons Dan and Jerry to bring the dining room table to the front yard, saying, "If Brother Keeble is eating out there, we are too." Alexander Campbell spoke against the wickedness of a system holding a man "guilty because his skin is a shade darker than the standard color of the times."[5] David Lipscomb candidly preached against racially segregated congregations existing in the same community, and added, "Not once did the apostles suggest that they should form separate congregations for the different races."[6]

---

[5] Alexander Campbell, *Christian Baptism* Vol. I (August, 1823), 18
[6] David Lipscomb, "Race Prejudice," *The Gospel Advocate*, Vol. XX. No. 8 (Feb. 21, 1878), 120

12. ARE CHRISTIANS GUILTY OF BEING INCONSISTENT IN HOW WE DEAL WITH RACISM?

Christians are like everyone else in that they can be and sometimes are inconsistent in dealing with various matters. This is certainly true regarding racism. Perhaps a few brief examples will suffice to illustrate this point. First, in past decades, Christians in America generally followed and enforced societal norms that segregated them from their brethren based on skin color while preaching and professing unity. At least some of that participation was not grudging. In some cases, Christians shared the racial hate that was common within substantial segments of American culture. Second, while American Christians are relatively persistent and vocal in speaking against certain spiritual and social ills, we have sometimes been silent regarding problems of racial hate and discrimination in our country and communities. Third, Christians today sometimes decry bigotry and racism as sinful but continue to celebrate brethren without qualification whom they know harbored and promoted racial bigotry and discrimination. These and similar behaviors are fairly labeled inconsistent or hypocritical, because faithful Christians know and teach that God is no respecter of persons and His people should not be respecters of persons either. In a culture riddled with inconsistencies regarding issues of race, Christians certainly are not immune to harboring and manifesting them. We should all be willing to confront our inconsistencies and earnestly strive to do better.

13. SHOULD CHRISTIANS TODAY REPENT AND APOLOGIZE FOR RACIAL PREJUDICES BOTH PAST AND PRESENT?

There are several published quotes from white church members seventy or eighty years ago that shock us for their blatant bigotry. Those hateful statements demanded an apology and repentance, and, from what we can tell, they were not always held accountable in their day. But all of those who made those statements seventy or eighty years ago are dead and have been for decades. Perhaps, there have been statements and writings, less prominent or well-preserved than some we might specifically mention, that were similarly sinful, and we denounce them all, no matter when they were made.

Apologies are essential to the functioning of the church. Jesus taught His disciples to leave their worship if they realized they had wronged someone: "Therefore if you bring your gift to the altar, and there remember that your brother has something against you, leave your gift there before the altar, and go your way. First be reconciled to your brother, and then come and offer your gift" (Matthew 5:24). But of course, the need for apologies in general when wrongs have been committed is not the question being addressed. The reason this question is in this book is well stated in a quote by Barclay Key in Daniel Blankenship's book *Race Relations in the Church of Christ During the Civil Rights Movement*, "While some positive changes have occurred since this era, in a collective sense, churches of Christ have failed to recognize and repent of their past racial sins."[7] Such statements that urge that the churches of Christ need to apologize for past racism are misguided and come from a misunderstanding of the organization of the church of the New Testament. Jesus referred to the universal church in Matthew 16:18, ("…on this rock I will build My church…") and that church is described

---

7   Daniel Blankenship, *Race Relations in the Church of Christ During the Civil Rights Movement* (Muskogee, OK: Breath of Life Press, 2012) 53

in and educated by the pages of the New Testament, but there simply is no vehicle for such an apology in the universal church. Who would presume to speak for the universal church? The church for which Christ died has no earthly headquarters, no spokesperson, no hierarchical system with a recognized head to make such declarations as does the Catholic church as well as various denominations. Each congregation of His church is autonomous, governed by elders (if they have qualified men), and made up of individual members. There is no occasion in Scripture where the universal church was urged to apologize to any person or group of people.

Is it true that through American history some white members of the church treated people of color in a sinful way? The historical record says yes, and we've read the quotes that make us shake our heads in shock and disappointment. White Christians today can disagree with those in the past who once sat in the pews we now occupy and can empathize with brethren who were hurt by them; however white Christians can no more apologize for them than a Christian of color can expect an apology from them for what happened in a different time. As Ezekiel 18:20 says, "The soul who sins shall die. The son shall not bear the guilt of the father, nor the father bear the guilt of the son. The righteousness of the righteous shall be upon himself, and the wickedness of the wicked shall be upon himself."

Jesus has taught us how to ask for forgiveness when we've wronged a brother (Matthew 18:15-17), how to forgive another (Luke 17:3), and how to restore one who has strayed from the teaching of Jesus (Galatians 6:1). But His Word doesn't allow for the universal church to express an apology for the sins committed by those who have died.

There were obviously racial problems in the past in congregations made up of people who are now dead and gone. No one today, black or white, can repent for those people or apologize for them; however, to the extent that people alive today maintain that racial division and are aware of doing so, repentance is certainly necessary.

14. WHERE DO WE DRAW THE LINE BETWEEN CULTURAL PREFERENCE AND SCRIPTURAL AUTHORITY?

This is an important question for Christians of all races. We all entered Christ's body as participants in a culture of one kind or another. Yet, in the metamorphosis of becoming a "new creature" (2 Corinthians 5:17), we already pledged a willingness to deny the culture of our upbringing if there is a biblical reason to do so. Christianity is a new life and new lifestyle. The culture of Christianity is the culture we must prioritize.

A paradox is a statement which, on its face, seems contradictory, yet it makes perfectly good sense. Here is a paradox: When people obey the Gospel, they maintain their ethnic heritage, and they *lose* their ethnic heritage. That may be paradoxical, but it isn't contradictory. There are things every man and woman must leave to enter the one body of Christ.

When the Grecian/Hellenistic widows were being neglected in the daily service to widows, the Apostles responded this way:

> Then the twelve summoned the multitude of the disciples and said, "It is not desirable that we should leave the word of God and serve tables. Therefore, brethren, seek out from among you seven men of good reputation, full of the Holy Spirit and wisdom, whom we may appoint over this business; but we will give ourselves continually to prayer and to the ministry of the word." And the saying pleased the whole multitude. And they chose Stephen, a man full of faith and the Holy Spirit, and Philip, Prochorus, Nicanor, Timon, Parmenas, and Nicolas, a proselyte from Antioch, whom they set before the apostles; and when they had prayed, they laid hands on them.
>
> Then the word of God spread, and the number of the

disciples multiplied greatly in Jerusalem, and a great many of the priests were obedient to the faith. (Acts 6:2-7)

The names of these seven (who appear to be deacons) reveal them to be Grecians. This demonstrates that it isn't necessarily wrong to acknowledge a Christian's nationality nor to use it to the benefit of the church and to the glory of our Lord. That is what happened here. So far as we know, no one felt slighted by the fact that only Grecian men were selected by the church, because they were Christians whose hearts were one (1 Corinthians 1:10) and their chief aim was to glorify Christ in the church.

It is also the case that we *lose* our ethnicity when we come into Christ's body: "For as many of you as were baptized into Christ have put on Christ. There is neither Jew nor Greek, there is neither slave nor free, there is neither male nor female; for you are all one in Christ Jesus" (Galatians 3:27-28). Christians may be diverse in many ways, but in Christ we are all spiritually uniform.

When people ask what we are (religiously), the answer would not be, "I'm a white Christian" or "I'm a brown Christian," but just "I'm a Christian." People's color is only skin deep. On the inside we are all washed in red. We are red with the blood of our Savior who saved us equally. All Christians must have this in common: Whenever we reference "our people," we are speaking of the members of Christ's body rather than our distinct ethnic groups. Christians are "our people."

15. IS IT WRONG FOR THERE TO BE A PREDOMINANTLY "WHITE CHURCH" AND "BLACK CHURCH" IN THE SAME CITY?

Jesus prayed that His disciples would be united (John 17:20-21). Paul encouraged the Christians in Corinth to be united in the same mind and in the same judgment (1 Corinthians 1:10). Christians are to give every effort to maintain the spirit of unity in the bond of peace (Ephesians 4:1-3). The church is to work together to the glory of God whether the congregation is predominantly "white" or "black." However, we must keep in mind that Jesus and Paul stress that we are to actually be unified and not to simply *look* unified. Just because people of different races or cultures are in the same building does not mean that unity has been achieved. Likewise, presenting the church (or body) as unified while still meeting separately based on color also hinders true unity. When there are two congregations of predominantly different races in relatively close proximity we should ask why. Sometimes there are doctrinal reasons why the division exists. We cannot compromise doctrinal truth in order to join hands with those of different races (2 John 9-11).

However, if we are simply divided into different congregations and ignoring each other because we are comfortable in our separation, this is sinful and goes against the prayer of Jesus in the Garden (John 17). There have been churches who have recently seen the need to merge and have decided to do so.[8] David Lipscomb was correct to point out that the Apostles admonished Jews and Gentiles in the first century to unity, forbearance, love, and brotherhood in Christ Jesus. He concluded it was sinful to have two congregations in the same communities for persons of separate and distinct races.[9] In the spirit of New Testament Christianity, we should seriously evaluate the reasons for having two congregations in

---
8 Bobby Ross, Jr., "Delaware churches—one white, one black—find new life by merging," *Christian Chronicle*, 25 Feb 2019
9 David Lipscomb, "Race Prejudice," *The Gospel Advocate*, Vol. XX. No. 8 (Feb. 21, 1878), 120

close proximity that are predominantly "white" or "black." Merging would be difficult and challenging, but this must not stop us from having these conversations and doing so where we can.

The New Testament calls us for us to be unified, to be one, and to love one another. While two congregations can be separate in location and still be obeying the New Testament command of unity, we must not settle for what is comfortable. If we preach that there is one body, we should model that by unifying congregations that are divided merely by racial and cultural differences (Ephesians 4:4). Paul spent his entire ministry urging Jews and Gentiles to be together and not allow cultural differences to divide them. A part of the glory of the gospel is God's ability to save all races of people in one body with one Savior (Ephesians 3:1-6). We should not accept Christ's body being divided by race or culture, which the New Testament admonishes us against and explicitly condemns. If there are two congregations in close proximity divided by color, we should do everything we can to be together. Sometimes there is enough distance between two congregations and the city is big enough to justify both congregations' existence, but this is not always the case. Later in the book we address how congregations might go about the process of merging two congregations, but we must first have the heart and desire to be together and do what pleases the Lord. Jesus Himself said that this warm, loving atmosphere would let the world know we are His disciples (John 13:34-35).

16. HOW SHOULD CHRISTIANS VIEW "CRITICAL RACE THEORY" IN PURSUING IMPROVED RACE RELATIONS?

Critical Race Theory (CRT), according to the *Encyclopedia Britannica*, is "the view that race, instead of being biologically grounded and natural, is socially constructed and that race, as a socially constructed concept, functions as a means to maintain the interests of the white population that constructed it."[10] CRT is a complex system of conjectures that emerged in the second half of the 20th century designed to call attention to the subtler forms of racial prejudice that replaced the more obvious forms of racism previously exposed by the American Civil Rights Movement. Proponents of CRT tend to see Western society as having institutionalized racism by making "whiteness" as normative,[11] and that "color-blind" laws actually disenfranchise some and privilege others.[12] A key tenant of CRT is that the laws of Western society constitute a mere human framework designed to serve the ruling class and nothing more.[13] Furthermore, CRT is founded on the assumption that epistemology is based primarily on history and life circumstances—that an individual's life situation cannot be adequately understood by anyone else who does not share the same socio-economic status.

As Christians, here are five of the reasons we reject CRT as a basis for improving race relations:

First, Christians must understand that right and wrong are not fluid, abstract ideas determined by a so-called privileged class of people. Rather, truth is fixed, orderly, and our world was spoken into existence by God (cf. Genesis 1:1; Psalm 33:6; John 1:1-3; 2 Peter 3:5; Hebrews 1:1-2; 11:3). Justice belongs to God, and human government is

---

10 Tommy Curry, "Critical Race Theory," *Encyclopedia Britannica*, 28 May 2020
11 Matt Mullins, "Is Critical Race Theory 'Unchristian'? Part 4, *Kingdom Diversity*, 30 May 2019
12 Mullins
13 Duncan Kennedy, "Antonio Gramsci and the Legal System," *ALSA Forum* Vol. VI. No. 1 (1982), 36

ordained by God to enforce the timeless morality written by God throughout nature (Romans 2:12-16). Truth and principles of justice are concrete and apply to all men consistently regardless of ethnicity, gender, age, wealth, and culture. God will judge the authorities who pervert justice, and justice is a knowable and timeless construct (Psalm 82:1-7). Truth and ethics are principles that are the same for everyone (cf. John 17:17) regardless of time and are not relative to those society deems privileged or subjugated.

Second, Christians must not assume there is treachery or malicious intent behind every law. "Do not call conspiracy all that this people calls a conspiracy, and do not fear what they fear" (Isaiah 8:12). Government exists to protect the innocent and judge the guilty—a task that is not an impossible feat (Romans 13:1-7). While we pursue justice for all men within the realm of our ability, we are at peace, knowing that final justice ultimately belongs to God (Romans 12:17-21). We must weigh the evidence before jumping to the conclusion that there is injustice in a given instance (Proverbs 18:13).

Third, Christians recognize that it is possible to be impartial, and we must strive for this. Otherwise, the biblical command to be impartial is impossible to achieve. "You shall do no injustice in court. You shall not be partial to the poor or defer to the great, but in righteousness shall you judge your neighbor" (Leviticus 19:15). If we judge all men by the standard of God's law, it is possible to be impartial.

Fourth, Christians know that truth is not relative to any particular people group. The Bible sufficiently equips us to be everything God expects us to be—as His children and as citizens (cf. 2 Timothy 3:16-17). The sum of God's Word is truth (Psalm 119:160). Jesus prayed, "Sanctify them by the truth, Your word is truth" (John 17:17). History, experience, and education help us "judge with right judgment" (John 7:24), but no one needs to be another ethnicity or gender to know the truth. Pride and a lack of concern for the truth, not ethnicity or privilege, are sins that keep individuals from knowing the truth.

Fifth, Christians know that CRT or any other social justice model can only change temporal policies. Racial reconciliation and social justice is always a noble pursuit, but apart from the ultimate goal of being reconciled to God, the usefulness of such a pursuit is limited. To believe man-made philosophies can achieve lasting societal change is nearsighted and naïve. The goal of true racial reconciliation can only be fully realized by changing hearts, not policies. We are not dedicated to a social gospel, just the *gospel*.

17. WHAT DOES THE BIBLE SAY ABOUT SLAVERY?

The subject of slavery is a vast topic in the Bible. Slavery is present in the both the Old and New Testaments.[14] Here are a few mentions in the Old Testament. Patriarchs possessed slaves and could purchase them with money (Genesis 17:23). The Israelites were slaves in Egypt and were undergoing hard servitude, which caused them to cry out to God for deliverance (Exodus 2:23-25). When the Law of Moses was given to Israel, there was much included within it about slaves and the treatment that they were to receive. If a master struck a slave and he died, the master was to be punished (Exodus 21:20). If a master destroyed the eye of a slave or knocked out his tooth, the slave was to be released (Exodus 21:26-27). The slaves of the Hebrews were to enjoy the Sabbath just like their masters (Exodus 23:12). If a Hebrew was enslaved to a fellow Hebrew, he was to be released after six years of service (Deuteronomy 15:12). A slave might desire to remain with his master after his six years of service; if he did, he was to have his ear "pierced" as a sign that he would be a slave to his master forever (Exodus 21:5-6). A slave could acquire freedom in several

---

[14] For an in-depth discussion on the slavery in both Testaments see: *The International Standard Bible Encyclopedia*, Volume 4: Q-Z, Wm. B. Eerdmans Publishing Co. (1988), 539-546

ways in Old Testament times (cf. Exodus 21:8; Leviticus 25:47-55). Much more could be said about slavery in Old Testament times, but these are a few samples.

Many Bible students are surprised to turn to the New Testament and see no outright condemnation of slavery as it was practiced in the first century Roman Empire. Everett Ferguson in his book *Backgrounds of Early Christianity* points out that slavery was a basic element in ancient society, and one in five of the residents in Rome was a slave.[15] Paul calls for Christians (including slaves) to abide in their calling (1 Corinthians 7:21-23). In Christ Paul says that Christians are all on the same level in the eyes of God whether they are slaves or free (Galatians 3:28-29; Colossians 3:11). Christian slaves are to obey their masters and do all of their work to the glory of God (Ephesians 6:5-8; Colossians 3:22-24). Even if masters were not kind and gentle, Christian slaves were to follow the example of Jesus and submit to those who were over them (1 Peter 2:18-25). The purpose for Christian slaves obeying their masters was so that the name of God would not be blasphemed (1 Timothy 6:1-2). Christian masters were told to treat their slaves fairly knowing that the ultimate Master is in heaven (Ephesians 6:9; Colossians 4:1).

The book of Philemon provides another discussion of slavery in the New Testament. Paul writes to a slave master (Philemon) about his runaway slave Onesimus who has been of help to Paul and has become a Christian (Philemon 10-11). Paul refers to the slave as his son and wants Philemon to receive him as a brother, even vowing to pay any debt that Onesimus may have (Philemon 12-19). Slavery was an institution that was in practice when the New Testament church came on the scene. The inspired Apostles did not seek to rid the Roman Empire of slavery but instead taught Christians how to live as slaves and masters in a world where slavery was a civil-endorsed institution. Paul does condemn kidnapping or stealing someone away in order to sell them off as property (1 Timothy 1:9-10). The slavery

---

[15] Everett Ferguson, *Backgrounds of Early Christianity*, Wm. B. Eerdmans Publishing Co. (1993), 56-58

that most Americans are familiar with is not entirely identical with the slavery found in the New Testament. The slavery practiced throughout America would fall under the condemnation of kidnapping given by Paul in 1 Timothy 1:9-10. Slavery in New Testament times was not based upon skin color; instead, people from various places and cultures were slaves. The Bible teaches masters that they must treat their slaves fairly and respect them as people made in the image of God (Genesis 1:26-27). It instructs Christian slaves to yield to their masters in a way that portrays Christ and promotes Christianity (1 Timothy 6:1-2; 1 Peter 2:18-21).

18. IS ALL SLAVERY THE SAME?

No, all slavery is not the same. Slavery was an accepted and widespread social institution in the ancient world, but it took various forms. At that time, a common practice was for people to be forced into servitude, perhaps as captives of war (e.g., 2 Kings 5:2ff). It was also common for debtors to be sold into servitude when they did not repay their debts (Exodus 22:2-3; Leviticus 25:39, 47; 2 Kings 4:1; Matthew 18:23-25). This latter arrangement was more akin to indentured servitude, where a person worked for a period of time to pay off a legitimate debt.

Moreover, slavery in the Old and New Testaments differed substantially from chattel slavery that was practiced in the West during the 18th and 19th centuries. For example, both among the Jews and in the Roman culture of the first century, slavery was not necessarily perpetual (e.g., Leviticus 27:47-55), and people were not consigned to bondage merely because of their ethnicity. People of various racial and national backgrounds were slaves, and they sometimes held prominent positions (Genesis 15:2-4; 39:1-4). Manumission, the release from slavery, was not at all uncommon, and slaves sometimes received wages and could own property. Sometimes slaves intermarried with their master's family (1 Chronicles 2:34-35) and inherited property (Genesis 15:2-3).

No, all slavery is not the same. Concepts and conditions of slavery have varied over time and across cultures. Yet Scripture is still sufficient in instructing Christians today who have encountered racial tension in America in the right attitudes we are to hold.

19. IS ABORTION AS PROMOTED IN THE U.S. TODAY AN EXAMPLE OF RACISM?

Yes. While we do not believe women who seek abortions are practicing racism, we believe the pro-abortion movement is guilty of racism. Black women are far more likely to get an abortion than women of another ethnic background. According to one popularly cited study, roughly one third of all aborted babies are black.[16] According to LifeNews.com, 79% of all Planned Parenthood clinics (the largest abortion provider in America) are located in predominately black and Hispanic neighborhoods.[17] Something appears to be very much amiss.

Charles Darwin's 1859 book *The Origin of Species* was subtitled *The Preservation of Favored Races in the Struggle for Life*. Darwin thought that some races of humans were evolutionarily superior to others, and he more directly taught that belief in his second major work on evolutionary theory, *The Descent of Man and Selection in Relation to Sex* published in 1871. Margaret Sanger, the founder of what became known as Planned Parenthood, spoke of sterilizing those she designated as "unfit." In her first handbook entitled *What Every Boy and Girl Should Know* (1915), she claimed that those in poverty and who lacked what she felt was adequate education should not be permitted to

16 Rachel Jones, "Characteristics of U.S. Abortion Patients, 2008, *Guttmacher Institute*
17 Steven Ertelt, "79% of Planned Parenthood Abortion Clinics Target Blacks, Hispanics," *LifeNews.com*, 16 Oct 2012

have children.[18] The idea that Margaret Sanger believed that black people and the poor were "unfit" to reproduce is hard to refute.

20. SHOULD CHRISTIANS IN THE WORSHIP ASSEMBLY CELEBRATE LEADERS IN THE HISTORICAL AMERICAN RESTORATION MOVEMENT, MLK JR. DAY, BLACK HISTORY MONTH, OR OTHER NATIONAL PUBLIC FIGURES?

There are matters of judgment where Christians will see things differently. Paul said that some would celebrate different days and events for cultural purposes while others might abstain (Romans 14:3-6). Christians can choose to celebrate holidays that honor certain leaders or even certain months that honor an entire group of people (i.e. Black History Month, Juneteenth, Hispanic Heritage Month, etc.). These days should be looked at in the same light as the Fourth of July, Thanksgiving, or any other man-made holiday. The Christian does not have to participate, but those who choose to celebrate are free to do so. While exercising our Christian liberty, we must also be careful not to become a stumbling block to others, and we should keep in mind the weak consciences of others (cf. 1 Corinthians 8:7-13; Galatians 5:13-14). Even though honoring those deserving of honor is always right (Romans 13:7), caution must be exercised when it comes to these special days or others like them. Individuals are free to observe days or months as he or she is persuaded in their own mind and should not bind their observance on others (Romans 14:5).

Similarly, Christians who were involved with restoring New Testament

---

18 Clenard Childress, Jr, "The Truth About Margaret Sanger," *BlackGeneocide.org*

Christianity should be honored and applauded, but they must not be worshipped (cf. Philippians 2:29). Men like Alexander Campbell, Barton Stone, "Racoon" John Smith and others did good things, but we must be reminded that they are just men. We can acknowledge the good that these individuals have done without making them the focus of our Bible class or worship service.

We should keep in mind that the local congregation does not have the right to make any of these celebrations and special days congregation-wide or turn them into a church observance (Galatians 4:9-11; Colossians 2:16-17). The local assembly is not a time to honor our country, race, or favorite historical figure. Regardless of how noble or respectable we might think a certain individual or group of individuals to be, we must be sure to keep things in their proper perspective (Acts 10:25-26; Revelation 19:10). The congregation assembles to worship and honor God (John 4:24; Acts 10:25-26; Revelation 22:9). God alone is worthy of our worship (Revelation 4:11; Deuteronomy 6:13-14).

21. IS IT OKAY TO SOMETIMES SPEAK IN BROAD GENERALITIES ABOUT PEOPLE GROUPS?

Yes, it is sometimes acceptable to speak in broad generalities about people groups. Several times in the New Testament, Jesus Himself spoke in broad generalities. Jesus rebuked the scribes and Pharisees in general though there were some who were not hypocritical impostors (i.e. Nicodemus; Matthew 23; cf. John 3:1-8). He also referred to tax collectors in general terms as He made points within the Sermon on the Mount (Matthew 5:46-47). When Paul quoted a poet from Crete who spoke about the immoral behavior of the Cretans, he agreed with the generality being made about the people of

Crete (Titus 1:12-13). While there are no doubt exceptions to generalities, such generalities are often useful when discussing behavior that may be prominent among certain groups of people (cf. Romans 2). When speaking in broad generalities, we should be mindful of exceptions and not hide behind generalities in an effort to mistreat others (cf. Luke 7:39; 15:1-2).

Furthermore, Christians must be sure that everything we do is done with the Golden Rule in mind, as we treat others in the same way we want to be treated (Matthew 7:12). It is important to keep in mind that generalities can be unfair and offensive. For instance, most white people, including white Christians, would be highly and rightly offended if a black person said, "White people are racist." Likewise, most black people, including black Christians, would be highly and righty offended if a white person said, "Black people are lazy." Imagine if someone, whether the person is a Christian or not, said, "Christians are hypocrites." Most Christians would object strongly. *We* would object strongly! Are there white racists? Sure there are. Are there lazy black people? Sure there are. Are Christians sometimes hypocritical? Absolutely. But sweeping generalizations, particularly negative generalizations, are sometimes nothing more than prejudices and tend to put others in the unfair and unenviable position of proving a negative, i.e., that they are "not" something. Even though it is not necessarily wrong to speak in broad generalities, we should be very careful in doing so. It can be *instrumentally* wrong.

22. TO WHAT EXTENT CAN CHRISTIANS BE INVOLVED IN SOCIAL ACTIVISM? IN CIVIL DISOBEDIENCE?

We define social activism as any effort to promote, impede, direct, or intervene in social justice reform. Regarding civil disobedience, we find both a broad and a narrow definition. It is not uncommon for civil disobedience to be loosely defined as the refusal to obey certain laws, demands, or orders by a governing body or representative in the name of a higher cause. In today's popular vernacular, even some forms of rioting are sometimes called civil disobedience. However, we believe civil disobedience must be more accurately defined as *nonviolent* or *peaceful*—that is, if it is to qualify as *civil*.

We see some clear principles in the Bible that directly relate to both social activism and civil disobedience. Generally speaking, civil disobedience is only permitted when following the government's laws would be a violation of God's laws (Acts 5:29). Bear in mind—as citizens and priests of another nation (1 Peter 2:9)—Christians answer to a higher law (Acts 5:29). As such, Christianity is often counter-cultural. Our values and moral ethics (e.g. sexuality, gender roles, work ethic, faith, etc.) are often at odds with the world. We walk by faith, not by sight (2 Corinthians 5:7).

We believe the "don't-tread-on-me" attitude—a virtue celebrated among citizens of the United States—can often be difficult to reconcile with the "go-the-second-mile" attitude commanded by our King (Matthew 5:38-48; cf. Proverbs 20:22; 24:29; Romans 12:17-19; 1 Thessalonians 5:15; 1 Peter 2:20-23; 3:9). Since the Bible is true, then looting (i.e. theft, swindling), the destruction of property (i.e. selfishness, rivalries), rioting (i.e. fits of anger, dissension, insolence), and "such things" (Galatians 5:21) are all sinful, and participating in these things will keep us out of heaven (cf. Matthew 7:12; Ephesians 5:3; Galatians 5:19-21; 1 Corinthians 6:10; 1 Timothy 1:9-11; Romans 1:28-32). If anything called social activism or civil disobedience involves these things, then Christians cannot be involved.

Furthermore, Christians of every worldly nation are duty-bound to be submissive to their civil authorities, even if those authorities are cruel and unjust (Luke 20:25; Romans 13:1-7; 1 Peter 2:13-17; 1 Timothy 2:1-2; Titus 3:1). After all, Paul wrote Romans 13 to Christians in Rome during the reign of the wicked emperor Nero (the one who would soon crucify

Christians and light them on fire to illuminate the streets of the city at night). In view of the biblical principles that we have just referenced, we believe it would have been scripturally questionable for a Christian to have participated in, for example, the Boston Tea Party—one of the most famous acts of civil disobedience in American history.

As it relates to committing civil disobedience in the name of racial activism, we recognize there is a degree of judgment as to where Christians should draw the line. Specific circumstances vary: civil laws and regulations sometimes contradict one another, governing authorities themselves sometimes break the law, etc. If the answer is not obvious in a specific instance, we recommend seeking the counsel of your congregation's shepherds (Hebrews 13:17). The principle remains, however, that our primary citizenship is not of this world. Paul told the Corinthians that if a Christian can follow civil law in gaining freedoms and rights (specifically in reference to slavery and subjugation), then he may "avail the opportunity" with God's consent (1 Corinthians 7:20-22). Notice, however, that Christians are only authorized to work within the parameters of the law—not circumvent or disregard the law.

Christians can be content even in an unjust society knowing this life is but a vapor (James 4:14). Every instance of injustice in this world will be met with the fury and judgment of God (Romans 12:17-21). This should bring us both comfort and fear. We must be praying for governments, leaders, and policymakers. "First of all, then, I urge that supplications, prayers, intercessions, and thanksgivings be made for all people, for kings and all who are in high positions, that we may lead a peaceful and quiet life, godly and dignified in every way" (1 Timothy 2:1-2, ESV). Do not underestimate the power of prayer in response to unjust government policies.

23. CAN CHRISTIANS BE INVOLVED IN PROTEST? IF SO, WHAT MUST BE THE PARAMETERS?

Christians are free to be involved in peaceful protest. A protest is simply a statement or action expressing disapproval of or objection to something. As Christians see unrighteousness in the world, one of the ways we can combat such is by exercising our right to protest peacefully (Romans 12:18; Hebrews 12:14). We must be careful to make a distinction between rioting and protesting. Sometimes as a peaceful protest is taking place, there will be some who attend and begin to riot. A riot is a violent disturbance of the peace by a crowd (cf. Acts 17:1-9; 19:21-41). Riots are sometimes accompanied by looting, which people cannot engage in with the approval of God (1 Corinthians 6:9-11). Christians can protest injustice peacefully, but they should do everything possible to distance themselves from those rioting and looting so as not to have their good be evil spoken of (cf. Romans 14:16). For instance, Christians may have to leave a protest if it turns violent or looters abound (1 Thessalonians 5:22). Likewise, Christians must not view protest as synonymous with riots—they are two separate things. Paul used his right as a Roman citizen to protest the accusations made against him by the Jews and he appealed to Caesar (Acts 25:11). Likewise, Christians can exercise their constitutional right to protest as long as they do so with the spirit of Jesus Christ and in a way that communicates honor and submission to God's appointed civil authorities (1 Corinthians 10:31).

24. IS THE ISSUE OF REPARATIONS A BIBLICAL MATTER OR A PURELY SOCIAL MATTER? WHAT DOES THE BIBLE SAY ABOUT IT?

When the Bible addresses the issue of reparations or restitution, it is normally in reference to individuals righting personal wrongs (cf. Leviticus 5:16; Numbers 5:5-10). Jesus encountered Zacchaeus (a tax collector) in Jericho, and as a result Zacchaeus restored four-fold of the things he had gotten by defrauding others (Luke 19:1-10). God did promise Israel that the Egyptians would be plundered as the Israelites depart from Egypt; these may or may not be viewed as reparations being paid to Israel (cf. Exodus 11:1-3; 12:33-36). For the most part, the Bible's discussion of repayment for wrongdoing involves individuals and not nations, though there may be a few exceptions.

Men like Ta-Nehisi Coates have made strong cases for the United States to give reparations to people of color but Coates does not speak on behalf of Christians.[19] Christians should always provide restitution where possible for wrongs that they have committed as individuals. Likewise, as it relates to political opinions on these matters, each individual should vote or express his or her opinion in love while prioritizing the unity of the Spirit among brethren (Ephesians 4:1-3). If the United States government ever decides that reparations should be paid, then Christians should comply rather than engage in "civil disobedience" (cf. Romans 13:6-8). If individual Christians seek reparations from the United States government, then that is an individual matter and must not be the cause of division in the church.

---

[19] Ta-Nehisi Coates, *We Were Eight Years in Power: An American Tragedy*, One World Publishing (2017), 163-208

25. HOW SHOULD A CHRISTIAN RESPOND TO RELIGIOUS GROUPS THAT HAVE RACIAL SUPREMACY BUILT INTO THEIR TEACHINGS?

There are a few religious groups that are founded on racist convictions. Black Hebrew Israelites (also called Hebrew Israelites, Black Jews, or African Hebrew Israelites) are a collection of religious networks and congregations who believe that those with black skin are the descendants of Israel. They claim to be Israelites, but their religion is not particularly Jewish. Instead, their religion is a hodgepodge of Holiness/Pentecostal, Freemasonry, Judaism, the occult, Mind Power, and Theosophy, among other religions.[20] Though Hebrew Israelites are not monolithic, there are a few beliefs that are central to their identity. They believe that white people are particularly evil, that black people are descendants of the Israelites, that Jesus is not God, and that black people will be saved by observing elements of the Mosaic Law.

The Nation of Islam, or Black Muslim movement, is a pseudo-Islamic religion. It incorporates aspects of Scientology and many ideas common to black nationalists. Core to the group's philosophical foundation is the idea that black men are gods and that white people were created by an evil black god (Yakub) who was a scientist.

There are other groups that practice either "white" or "black" supremacy that we have not taken the time to address. Surely the Mormon church and some Christian groups have historically made racial supremacy a key tenet of their belief system. As it relates to our purpose, what these groups (and others like them) have in common is the belief that ethnicity is key to your salvation. It is not uncommon for impressionable young people to become enamored with these groups after coming under the influence of a family member or mentor. These groups—many of them have cult-like

---

[20] Jacob Dorman, "Black Israelites aka Black Jews aka Black Hebrews," *Introduction to New and Alternative Religions in America*, 59

characteristics—appeal to their felt needs and sense of purpose.

How should Christians respond? First, we should seek out children born into at-risk homes and find ways to model Christian care, love, and affirmation. "By this, all will know that you are My disciples, if you have love for one anther" (John 13:34-35). Children need to find support among God's people; otherwise they will seek affirmation elsewhere. Second, Christians should study the specific doctrines of these groups and learn how to contend for the faith, if anyone we know (a friend or family member) should fall under the influence of someone from one of these groups. Third, we should teach that Jesus is God (cf. John 10:30) and that no one can come to the Father except through obedience to Him (John 14:6). Fourth, we remind our friends and family members that God is not a respecter of persons (Acts 10:34)—God does not favor one people group over another. Every human being is made in the image of God (Genesis 1:26-27). Ethnicity does not gain us any kind of righteous standing before God (Ephesians 2:11-22; Romans 8:14; 9:30-33).

26. WHEN IS IT RIGHT FOR CHRISTIANS TO DISTANCE THEMSELVES FROM THE VALUES OF THEIR OWN ETHNIC CULTURES?

In short, Christians should distance themselves from the values of their particular ethnic cultures when those cultural values conflict with Christian values. Whether by birth or personal choice, each individual belongs to a myriad of groups that afford varying degrees of safety, support, satisfaction, and self-realization. Since every individual is part of more than one group, there is always a possibility of tensions when one group's interests and ideals do not align perfectly with another group's interests and ideals.

Paul addressed this dynamic in the book of Philippians when he wrote, "Only let your manner of life be worthy of the gospel of Christ: that, whether I come and see you or be absent, I may hear of your state, that ye stand fast in one spirit, with one soul striving for the faith of the gospel" (Philippians 1:27, ASV). The Greek verb translated "manner of life" (ASV, ESV), "conversation" (KJV), or "conduct" (NKJV, NIV) in English versions of the Bible, is very closely related to the English words *politics* and *political* and literally means "live as citizens." In using this word, Paul drew on the Philippians' national allegiance and affection for Rome and charged them to redirect that allegiance to their heavenly citizenship. His overarching directive to the church at Philippi was for its members to conduct themselves foremost as citizens of God's spiritual commonwealth governed by the gospel of Jesus Christ rather than as privileged citizens of mighty Rome as they had before. Rather than reveling in their common identity with the Romans, they were to live in communion with fellow Christians. They were "fellow citizens" with the saints and members of God's household (cf. Ephesians 2:19). This was the group to which they primarily belonged and with whom they needed to primarily associate.

Christians are not immune to the pressures of simultaneously belonging to multiple groups. Their national, ethnic, and spiritual interests, for example, will sometimes conflict, so it can be dangerous for Christians to hold too closely to the values of any group whose values are not specifically informed by the doctrine of Christ. It is particularly important that church leaders, like elders and preachers, examine themselves to ensure that they do not conflate ethnic and spiritual values and that they are intentional about helping members to understand the difference as well.

27. WHAT IS SYSTEMIC RACISM? WHAT IS WHITE PRIVILEGE? WHAT ROLE SHOULD THESE TERMS PLAY IN CHRISTIAN DISCUSSIONS ABOUT RACE RELATIONS IN THE CHURCH?

Systemic racism can be defined as a form of racism that is embedded as normal practice within a society or organization. Undeniable examples of systemic racism from American history include slavery and the Jim Crow laws of segregation. There is a lot of discussion today about whether systemic racism is still present in the United States. There are often statistics cited and shared in an effort to show either that it still exists though exercised in different ways or that it no longer is an issue. The writers of this book do not all agree on the issue of systemic racism in American culture. However, we do agree that racism is always wrong, and where it is seen and practiced, it must be condemned and corrected (Matthew 22:37-40; 1 John 4:20-21). Whether one believes that racism is systemic or that similar cases of racial injustice are merely coincidental, the Christian's responsibility to the behavior does not change. Sometimes Christians engage in heated debates over whether or not racism is systemic, but we do not have to agree or come to identical conclusions on these matters in order to be pleasing to God. As long as we do not tolerate or approve of bigotry or injustice, our understandings about the specific definition or extent of "systemic racism" must not be allowed to divide or used to divide the body.

In the context of American culture, the phrase "white privilege" is a shorthand way of referring to social advantage that a person automatically inherits simply by being white, i.e., a Caucasian. Some deny that there is any privilege or advantage enjoyed by Caucasian people, while others insist that such is prevalent. Again, the writers are not in lock-step agreement on white privilege and its prevalence or lack thereof in American society. Christians must not cause division over whether or not white people are privileged in American culture in some ways. Christians are equal in the body of Christ and must not prefer any race above another, in or out of the church (Galatians 3:26-29; James 2:1-13).

Seeing that terms like systemic racism and white privilege are not biblical terms but rather social terms, Christians will not all see these things the same. *We should not divide the church over words on which we don't agree* (1 Timothy 6:4; 2 Timothy 2:14) *or insist people see things in society just as we see them.* We must only be bound by Scripture. What Christians must view the same is righteousness and unrighteousness. What God approves we must approve and what God condemns we must condemn. *We may use different terms or refuse to use certain terms, but we can still be united and glorify God in the process* (John 17:20-21).

28. DOES SCRIPTURE DISCOURAGE INTERRACIAL MARRIAGE?

No. Consider Rahab, who was a Canaanite woman. Yet she is found in the Christ's genealogy found in Matthew 1. That means she—a Canaanite, a descendent of Canaan—must have married an Israelite—a descendent of Shem. However, unlike the ungodly Canaanite people she came from, Rahab is commended for her faith in God (Hebrews 11:31). Similarly, Ruth was a Moabite. Yet she is also found in the Matthew 1 genealogy, meaning she married an Israelite. Before she married, however, she expressed faith in the true God (Ruth 1:16).

We understand that there are still some who believe that interracial marriage is wrong. Some would claim that Deuteronomy 7:3-4 condemns such a union. Yet, in this passage, God is forbidding the Israelites (and only the Israelites) from entering into an interracial marriage *for religious reasons*.

The nations surrounding the Israelites were pagans and idolaters, and God knew the Israelites would be led astray if they intermarried with them. (Incidentally, the people in the surrounding nations probably had a similar skin color as the Israelites.)

Christians are given the same principle in 2 Corinthians 6:14. We are not to be "unequally yoked" with unbelievers. While a religiously mixed marriage is not grounds for divorce (1 Corinthians 7:12), serious Christians must avoid marrying non-Christians (cf. 1 Corinthians 7:39).

The irony is that those who condemn interracial marriage sometimes have less discomfort with Christians marrying non-Christians. They have their priorities completely backward. The fact that some within Christendom are opposed to interracial marriage (but not inter-religious marriage) is the real shame. Without hesitation, we (the authors of this book) would rather our children marry faithful Christians of a different ethnicity than a Christians of the same ethnicity with marginal faith. In fact, we wouldn't just "rather" our child marry the person with a different skin color in that instance; we would strongly encourage it.

29. WHAT ROLE SHOULD RACE PLAY IN THE SELECTION OF ELDERS IN A CONGREGATION TODAY?

In Acts 6 when the Grecian widows were being neglected by the church, men were sought out by the church to ensure that the problem was corrected. Judging by the names of the men selected for the task, the church felt it best to select Grecian men. The important thing to observe, however, is that the guidelines for the selection said nothing about nationality. The criteria was this: "Therefore, brethren, seek out from among you seven men of good reputation, full of the Holy Spirit and wisdom, whom we may appoint over this business" (Acts 6:3).

It was not wrong to choose men who were Grecians to care for the Grecian widows: in fact, there was probably an obvious benefit. But it would have been wrong to make that the chief characteristic of the men to the neglect of what the Apostles actually required ("...of good reputation, full of the Holy Spirit and wisdom").

Similarly, there are clear advantages to having men of different nationalities serving together as elders, but it would be sinful to ordain a man to this important role solely because of the color of his skin while neglecting the scriptural qualifications given in 1 Timothy 3:1-7 and Titus 1:5-9. None of the Holy Spirit's qualifications for elders references race. Our Lord is concerned about righteousness and wisdom. Likewise, it would also be sinful to resist ordaining a man who does meet the scriptural qualifications simply because of the color of his skin.

30. HOW DO I RESPOND TO THE ARGUMENT THAT CHRISTIANITY IS THE "WHITE MAN'S RELIGION"?

When some contend that Christianity is the "white man's" religion, it should be noted that Christianity began in Jerusalem almost 2,000 years ago (Acts 2). The accusation that Christianity is a white man's religion is sometimes levied by non-whites who reject Christianity because of people in previous generations who claimed to be Christians while manipulating Bible texts to uphold chattel slavery and racial supremacy in America. Christianity does not belong to any race in particular, and men and women of all races regardless of who they are or where they are from can can become Christians. When Peter preached the first gospel sermon, Jews from all nations were present to hear the gospel (Acts 2:9-11). Soon the disciples were scattered throughout Judea and Samaria preaching the Word (Acts 8:4). Philip taught a man from Ethiopia the gospel and he became a Christian very early on in the church's history (Acts 8:26-40). One who claims that white men started Christianity is clearly misinformed about biblical Christianity and must be shown with patience, kindness, and love that Christianity was begun by Jesus of Nazareth who lived in Palestine and died for all men to be saved (Matthew 26:28; 2 Timothy 2:24-26). Anyone who fears God and does what is right is accepted by Him regardless of the color of his or her skin (Acts 10:34-35).

31. WHAT IS MICROAGGRESSION? HOW SHOULD IT AFFECT INDIVIDUALS IN THE CHURCH?

Consider a few results of this Google search: "Define microaggression."

> A subtle but offensive comment or action directed at a minority or other non-dominant group that is often unintentional or unconsciously reinforces a stereotype: microaggressions such as "I don't see you as black." (*dictionary.com*)

> A comment or action that subtly and often unconsciously or unintentionally expresses a prejudiced attitude toward a member of a marginalized group (such as a racial minority). (*Merriam-Webster Dictionary*)

> A statement, action, or incident regarded as an instance of indirect, subtle, or unintentional discrimination against members of a marginalized group such as a racial or ethnic

minority. (*Lexico*)

In the context of how this relates to Christians or congregations, the question might be more clearly stated: "How should Christians respond to incidental slights or comments that may rub the wrong way, whether intentional or unintentional?"

The word *micro* is unfortunate. It was presumably coined to refer to times when people take small digs at people of color. We are confident that it sometimes happens in the church, but unfortunately, the very nature of the aggressions being micro (very small) leaves the door open to people subjectively misjudging the motives of statements and actions of others. If the aggression is unintended, are we always sure it exists? And what kind of atmosphere will this create in a church that is blessed to have a mixture of races in its assemblies? Racial division may be caused and unity may be lost because of real or perceived microaggressions.

Consider four different fictitious church members. Some—or all—of these may exist in your congregation:

1. Bill, a white man born in 1957, was reared in a home that was openly racist. It was always a given in his father's house that white people were superior to black people. As an adult and a Christian, Bill has made many changes in how he thinks and talks, especially around people of color. Nevertheless, there are still times when he's with black Christians in which he starts feeling light-hearted and overly-frank and becomes cavalier about their viewpoints. He will let remnants of his childhood surface and say—not in anger, but in thoughtlessness—hurtful things to his brothers and sisters. He doesn't regret such moments because he feels he is striking a righteous balance between how things were in the '60s and how they are now.

2. Sarah is a white sister born in 1959, reared in a home of dedicated and sincere Christians. Growing up through the racial unrest of the '60s, Sarah was often with black children. As a teen she would invite

black friends from school to come to worship with her and a couple of them were baptized. Today she is discouraged because no matter how hard she tries to meet the expectations of her black sisters, she never can. When she tries to talk with them about ways they feel slighted, she draws their wrath. When she questions any of their assertions about what things offend them, or the positions they take, she seems to make them angry. To Sarah, the relationships can feel hopeless to her.

3. Matthew is a black brother born in 1967 and is a dedicated Christian who was taught and obeyed the Gospel just before he and his wife married. He's a deacon in a racially mixed congregation. He loves his white brothers, but truth be told, there are times when they become so comfortable around him that they let their teasing become racially offensive. He lets it go. He knows they are good men, and he reasons that, after all, he has weaknesses of his own as a Christian. Still, that occasional feeling that they see him as somehow inferior because of the color of his skin hurts him. He wants to feel the total acceptance that he senses the white brothers feel in the church.

4. Mary, a black sister born in 1998, was reared by her parents to believe that all white people are naturally given to racism. She takes it for granted and is training her children to believe the same. Consequently, Mary is sensitive to things her brothers and sisters in Christ say that might reflect even the smallest slight to a person of color and, in her effort to make relations better, will always speak her mind. The frequency of these corrections has sadly created a distance between Mary and her white sisters who would like to be close to her. They have unfortunately grown to fear the awkwardness of being around her. They feel they just can't be careful enough to satisfy Mary, and that no matter how hard they try, she will judge them harshly.

We created these characters to illustrate the one-size-doesn't-fit-all facet of this discussion. The church is filled with diverse people who have unique temptations to sin (James 1:13-14). God's Word makes us complete and completely furnishes us to every good work (2 Timothy 3:16-17). We are to believe, follow, and defend that Word (Jude 3). That applies to the matter of race relations.

Scripture teaches forbearance—great patience—among Christians. As brothers and sisters who love the upcoming appearing of Jesus (2 Timothy 4:8), we must work hard to preserve unity in the body. We want to be known as the people who love one another, regardless of color (John 13:34). On one hand, each one of us, black, white, or brown, must administer the same reasonable care to protect one another's feelings, and that requires maturity and balance. On the other hand, some people in the church are insensitive and need to apply the Golden Rule for a change (Matthew 7:12).

Like Paul with Peter in Galatians 2, elders who identify a man like Bill (number one in the description above) should take him aside for a calm but frank talk in the interest of correcting his attitude and behavior. They should teach him the importance of creating a welcoming atmosphere for every penitent believer who attends and the need for his own personal growth toward seeing souls of brothers rather than skin tones. He should apologize to his black brethren. A Christian who is careless about slighting and hurting fellow Christians of any color will likely cause division and is bound to Scripture that binds us together in love and patience.

Mary's elders should also take the time to lovingly show her that presuming the thoughts of all white people is also a hinderance to Christian unity and is not "lov[ing] one another earnestly, for love covers a multitude of sins" (1 Peter 4:8). A Christian who develops a sort of hypersensitivity combined with a propensity to express hurt feelings among members will soon create division in the church, regardless of the color of his skin, and is also equally bound by Scripture that binds us together in love and patience.

It seems self-evident that in healthy interactions between Christians, both hypersensitivity and insensitivity are wrong. Both jeopardize our unity. Both violate the same Golden Rule and set the table for division based on race—the very thing we're hoping to prevent. Consider the following passages and how they speak to our subject in this question:

> But the fruit of the Spirit is love, joy, peace, longsuffering, kindness, goodness, faithfulness, gentleness, self-control. Against such there is no law. And those who are Christ's have crucified the flesh with its passions and desires. (Galatians 5:22-24)

> I, therefore, the prisoner of the Lord, beseech you to walk worthy of the calling with which you were called, with all lowliness and gentleness, with longsuffering, bearing with one another in love, endeavoring to keep the unity of the Spirit in the bond of peace. (Ephesians 4:1-3)

> Therefore, as the elect of God, holy and beloved, put on tender mercies, kindness, humility, meekness, longsuffering; bearing with one another, and forgiving one another, if anyone has a complaint against another; even as Christ forgave you, so you also must do. But above all these things put on love, which is the bond of perfection. And let the peace of God rule in your hearts, to which also you were called in one body; and be thankful. (Colossians 3:12-15)

> Love suffers long and is kind; love does not envy; love does not parade itself, is not puffed up; does not behave rudely, does not seek its own, is not provoked, thinks no evil; does not rejoice in iniquity, but rejoices in the truth; bears all things, believes all things, hopes all things, endures all things. (1 Corinthians 13:4-7)

Brothers and sisters in Christ don't carry chips on their shoulders. They see themselves as members of a body that was bought with blood (Ephesians 5:25), recipients of an unspeakable gift (2 Corinthians 9:15). They see their roles as giving praise and glory to our Lord while adorning the doctrine

(Titus 2:10). Where is the room in that picture for white Christians being nonchalant about abusing, in any small or large dose, members of color, or for members of color to be constantly on watch for small, unintended slights?

32. HOW SHOULD I PROCEED IF I HEAR SOMEONE IN THE CHURCH MAKE A RACIALLY OFFENSIVE COMMENT?

Private accusations of bigotry, or perhaps even racism, should be treated as we would treat any other such accusation, even if it had nothing to do with race. Jesus taught us that the offended Christian should go privately and personally to the offender and tell him his fault between the two of them alone:

> Moreover if your brother sins against you, go and tell him his fault between you and him alone. If he hears you, you have gained your brother. But if he will not hear, take with you one or two more, that "by the mouth of two or three witnesses every word may be established." And if he refuses to hear them, tell it to the church. But if he refuses even to hear the church, let him be to you like a heathen and a tax collector. (Matthew 18:15-17)

If the offender refuses to apologize or to explain sufficiently why this is all a misunderstanding, the offended Christian should take one or two others and revisit the matter. That second meeting is important because it adds substance to the accusation and establishes whether or not a sin has *actually been committed*. The Matthew 18 plan is our Lord's remedy for private sin between church members regardless of their color. What sometimes concerns us is the possibility of a member who, influenced by the world, makes a habit of raising small slights that have come from white Christians and reflexively believes them to be racially motivated. We aren't saying these slights shouldn't be addressed, but neither should they be constantly created in people's imaginations. Where will that spirit lead but to division in the body? The teaching of Jesus in Matthew 18 would go a long way to preventing such division.

That second meeting that our Lord taught in Matthew 18, where one or two others are brought to discuss the matter with the one accused of sin, could end in a variety of ways. The offender could repent, and the whole matter put to rest. The offended could be convinced that a sin has in fact not been committed, and the matter dropped. A plan could be made to take the matter to the assembly of the church, etc. Willful insensitivity or prejudice is a sin that is not special in this regard. If a Christian harms another because of racism, the harm must be stopped and the sinner corrected.

Matthew 18 concerns sins committed between individual Christians that are not public in nature. Should someone in the church make a public statement, say during worship or class, that plainly expresses bigotry, someone in authority should come before the church before the assembly is dismissed and express that this is not true to the values of the New Testament or this church.

33. IN WHAT SENSE SHOULD CHRISTIANS BE "COLOR-BLIND"? IN WHAT SENSE SHOULD THEY NOT?

The idea of being "color-blind," in terms of sociology, is an ideal society where race is insignificant and does not limit an individual's opportunities.[21] Christians should love and respect all people as image bearers of God (Genesis 1:26-27). All people come from Adam and Adam was formed by God (Genesis 5:1-2; Acts 17:26). There can be no mistake about it—the way God created this world shows that He intended that we all be valued equally. Christians should remember God does not show any partiality or favoritism based on race, and we should not either (Acts 10:34-35). In Christ racial, cultural, and gender distinctions still exist, but these distinctions do not make one person more valuable to God than another. We are all one in Christ (Galatians 3:26-29). If by "color-blind" one means that Christians should not treat anyone better or worse based on superficial distinctions like race, then the answer is yes, Christians must be color-blind (cf. James 2:1).

Still, we should be sure to appreciate that God did make various colors and people do not all look physically identical. God in His infinite wisdom has made us different shades and colors. Christians do not have to deny these realities in order to practice the impartial faith of James 2. Different races tend to have different cultural preferences and customs, and this is part of the greatness of the kingdom of God. God is able to save Jews, Gentiles, blacks, and whites through His Son Jesus Christ (Ephesians 2:14-16; 3:1-5). Jesus' blood destroys the differences that separate Jews and Gentiles, but one does not have to cease being a certain color in order to be a Christian. Some, in their attempt to stress their love for all people, profess to be "color-blind," but to be totally color-blind is impossible since God made us with color. Likewise, sometimes claiming to be color-blind fails to recognize unique challenges or problems of a certain group. For example, when

---
21 Ken Wytsma, *The Myth of Equality: Uncovering the Roots of Injustice and Privilege*, IVP Books (2017), 45

the Judaizing teachers were binding circumcision, this was a problem for Gentile Christians (Acts 15). It would do no good to claim to be color-blind and fail to see a problem uniquely affecting Gentiles. Sometimes because we live in a fallen world, people are treated differently because of the color of their skin and we cannot deny this or dismiss it by claiming that we are color-blind. We also should acknowledge the manifold wisdom of God in His creation of various colors and shades among the human race (Romans 11:33-34). If God did not want us to see and acknowledge color at all, He could have omitted it from His creation. Because He did not, we should not fail to acknowledge it. We should be sure not to treat people better or worse because of the color of their skin, but we also must not go as far as to deny that their skin has a certain color.

Seeing that occasionally it is right to acknowledge the color of another, we must be careful not to assume that a white person is racist if he makes mention of a "nice black family" or describes a baby as a "beautiful black baby." Just because race is noticed and mentioned does not necessarily mean racism or bigotry is being expressed. People are not color-blind in the sense that they cannot see color at all, so there are occasions when it will be mentioned. Still, the mention of a particular race must never be abused or mentioned in a derogatory way. White Christians should keep in mind that black people have often had their race highlighted in a condescending way to express negative ideas and this may affect how comments are received. Black Christians should be sure to think the best of their white brethren and not assume racism or insult where it is not present.

34. WHAT ROLE DOES/SHOULD ANECDOTAL EVIDENCE PLAY IN DISCUSSIONS OF RACISM?

Anecdotal evidence is evidence that is based upon an individual's personal experience. While anecdotal evidence is not the only thing that matters in discussions of race, it must not be dismissed. Paul used anecdotal evidence when he spoke about his former life as a Pharisee and his new life in Jesus Christ (Acts 22:1-21; 23:5-6). Paul's personal conversion account and his life as a Pharisee did not make his claims about the gospel more true, but it did help those he was speaking to appreciate where he was coming from.

In discussions on race, some people may claim that they have never experienced racism or never seen any instance of racism done to others. While this may be hard to believe, some have grown up in different cultures and have had different experiences. We are unwise to dismiss the actual experiences of others simply because we have not personally experienced them ourselves. Part of weeping with those who weep is learning what makes them weep and trying to see things from their perspective even if their perspective has not been our own (Romans 12:15). Anecdotal evidence must be weighed and sifted through, but it should be carefully considered.

Anecdotal evidence allows one to walk a mile in the shoes of his neighbor and appreciate the experiences of others. Experiences differ even among those from the same race, and therefore each person's anecdotal evidence will vary from person to person. When discussing racism, many may believe that certain behavior has ceased to be a problem but by talking to someone else may find that they are mistaken. Anecdotal evidence is obviously not free from bias and therefore cannot be the final verdict in discussions on racism, but discussions on racism that omit anecdotal evidence are lacking helpful and necessary information.

35. HOW CAN CHRISTIANS DISCUSS PROBLEMS OF RACISM WITHOUT DISRUPTING THE UNITY OF THE CHURCH? WHAT KINDS OF ATTITUDES ARE COUNTERPRODUCTIVE?

Christians can discuss problems of disunity as long as we remember to do so in love (1 Corinthians 16:14). We must be willing to see that we might be wrong and that someone else with a differing viewpoint might be right. If we possess the fruit of the Spirit and seek to live by the Christian graces, there is no subject that Christians cannot discuss and still maintain unity (Galatians 5:22-23; 2 Peter 1:5-8). Attitudes that are counterproductive are those where we give place to the devil through uncontrolled anger (Ephesians 4:26-27), when we are prideful or arrogant (Proverbs 16:18; 1 Peter 5:6), and when we fail to listen to each other (Proverbs 18:13). We cannot respond to problems in the world like the world responds (1 John 2:15-17). We must respond like those who have had their minds renewed by Jesus Christ (Romans 12:2; Ephesians 4:23).

Christians must not adopt the rules of the culture concerning racial discussions. Consider some examples of counterproductive assertions often heard today:

- A black person who says he/she has received racist, bigoted, or prejudicial treatment should be doubted, held in suspicion, or accused of playing the victim.
- White people can never do enough to prove they are not racist.
- Racism, prejudice, and bigotry are attitudes of all white people and they are unable to change.
- Black people should come to grips with the reality that slavery happened centuries ago and they need to get over it.
- There is no solution to the racial problems faced in the world, and

we must simply continue in endless dialogue and conversation but never say the problems can be solved.

Christians are commanded not to conform to the world but to be transformed by renewing their minds (Romans 12:2). Attitudes such as the ones mentioned above may not be explicitly spelled out by any group, but believing these creates an atmosphere where unity and healthy problem solving cannot take place. The church is the institution provided by Jesus to be the answer to human division of any kind (Ephesians 2:14-16). The church must be honest about the problems that exist, but the church must be the solution and not a part of the problem.

36. WHAT STEPS SHOULD CONGREGATIONS TAKE IN MERGING TWO CULTURALLY DISTINCT CONGREGATIONS?

Congregational mergers can be very beneficial. Ideally, they lead to more efficient use of the church's resources and greater synergies as more Christians cooperate together with their various skills and experiences. Merging congregations provides an added bonus in places where congregations have previously split because of sinful divisions, including personality conflicts and doctrinal errors. When congregations merge in areas that have a legacy like that, their display of unity and fellowship is certainly God-honoring and potentially creates a new and more positive legacy for the church and the community. The same is true where individual churches have been deliberately divided based on the disparate cultural background of their members.

When congregations attempt to merge, there will almost invariably be challenges. Leaders within the individual churches should pray and talk together about the challenges they can anticipate long before actually merging. In those discussions, some differences in doctrine, traditions, and preferences will be obvious while others will not. It may not be necessary to resolve every potential issue, but leaders should pursue as much resolution as possible and articulate some agreed-upon principles and methods for working cooperatively through unforeseen difficulties that might arise.

When congregations with cultural differences merge, each will likely have additional challenges to work through. Ideally, doctrinal differences should be privately sorted out among leaders so that they can be addressed with one voice when occasions warrant. It is also imperative that leaders help their separate groups to recognize the inevitability of differences, as well as the attendant discomfort, and understand the distinction between differences that are eternally important and those that are not. Also, before the congregations finally come together, they are wise to have a series of joint classes and assemblies to allow members to get a "feel" for one another and ease the transition. These joint meetings will undoubtedly provoke questions or concerns that might not be fully anticipated or appreciated otherwise. By taking progressive steps like this, the transition to becoming one congregation will likely be less traumatic and stressful for all parties involved.

Racial sensitivities and insensitivities are potentially major obstacles that can easily be underestimated. For instance, people tend to see others as hypersensitive, but the truth is that both black people and white people tend to be hypersensitive about racial matters. As a result, when racially disparate groups come together and interact in ongoing and personal ways, tensions can easily arise. In this connection, it is important to understand that, generally speaking, the sensitivities exist for different reasons. Black Christians are impacted by historical and ongoing discrimination or, at the very least, the perception of the same, both in society and in the church. Consequently, they can be particularly wary of racial slights. White

Christians are often afraid of being perceived as or labeled "racist" because of any comments, whether careless, thoughtless, or unknowing that they might make, and so they are often uncomfortable discussing race matters with black people, including their black brothers and sisters in Christ. These are not the only potentially problematic dynamics, but they are important ones that should not be ignored. Leaders should discuss these things and work to prepare members to be appropriately sensitive to one another and patient with one another. These things should not stop congregations from pursuing mergers, but their influence on potential success should not be underrated.

The idea of merging congregations can seem daunting, and the undertaking itself can be challenging. However, the potential benefits to the Lord's church and its influence are tremendous. Where mergers between culturally distinct congregations can benefit the work of the church and reverse the historical course of "separate but equal" among Christians, they should be diligently and carefully pursued.

37. WHAT IS THE ULTIMATE GOAL IN DISCUSSIONS OF RACIAL DIVISIONS?

The ultimate goal of such discussions should be reconciliation. The Bible says, "If it be possible, as much as in you lieth, be at peace with all men" (Romans 12:18, ASV). Obeying this directive requires, among other things, affirmative measures to address and overcome hostilities. Open, candid, and compassionate discussion is an important step toward reconciling people who are separated by the racial divisions that persist in American culture and in the Lord's church. They will not dissipate with the passing of time or merely because we pretend they no longer exist.

In addition to reconciling people to one another, discussions about racial divisions are necessary in reconciling people to God. First, to the extent that some harbor racial bigotries, participate in oppression, or perpetuate racial hatred, they must repent in order to be right with God. Christians should have the same goal in discussing this sin as they have in discussing any other. The discussions are inevitable in bringing some to repentance (Galatians 2:11-17; Acts 10:1-20). Second, they are integral for Christians to carry out the Great Commission. Jesus commands Christians to share the gospel with every creature in every nation (Matthew 28:19-20; Mark 16:15). This requires overcoming barriers like racial divisions (Acts 8:5, 25), and that often requires some discussion regarding the barriers (e.g., John 4:7-26; Acts 10:21-28).

SECTION 3

CONCLUSION

THE ROADMAP TO SOLVING RACIAL TENSIONS IN THE LOCAL CHURCH

Many good lessons have come from our discussions as we wrote this book. Some nights our meetings went long and seemed to accomplish only a little. Through the process we have all grown in our love and respect for one another. It is doubtful that racial tensions will ever be solved in the country; first, because the efforts to resolve them are sometimes counterproductive, and second, because some who are shouting the loudest may not really be offering a clear path to resolution. Endless, ongoing dialogue may be the goal of some.

But what about racial tensions in the local church of Christ? No sin in the New Testament was treated with endless dialogue. True resolution in any group of people requires a specific identification of the sin—something which is often missing in today's conversations in the church. In reality, racial division still lingers in the church of Christ in America in two specific areas. The two are these:

1. In communities which have a "black church" and a "white church" near one another. Neither of the congregations may consider this a problem or a racial conflict; they may be in full fellowship and simply prefer to have separate assemblies. We still doubt that this arrangement is completely consistent with Scripture (consider the words and implications of Galatians 2). Our hope is that reading of this book will motivate elders to start discussions about the merging of black and white churches. In ancient times there would have been nothing wrong with a Gentile town like Ephesus having a Gentile church. Neither would there be anything wrong with a Jewish town like Jerusalem having a

Jewish church. But in view of passages such as Galatians 2, would the Holy Spirit have objected to having Gentile and Jewish churches of Christ only a short distance apart in the same town?

2. In individual hearts and lives. It is important to acknowledge that Christians, like non-Christians, can and do struggle with racial prejudice, bias, and bigotry. While we are convinced it is uncommon, there are some church members, whether black or white or brown, who hold enmity toward their brothers and sisters who are racially different from them. *Systemic* racism does not exist in the Lord's church today, but individual Christians are tempted by their own lusts (James 1:13-15). Sometimes a man's strong temptation to sin is saying or doing incendiary or unkind things.

The Lord didn't see fit to create a world-wide governing body over elderships. If He had, and you were asked to propose the solution to racism in His church world-wide today (other than mere/perpetual dialogue), consider some things your solution would include.

From our pulpits and classes, we must encourage one another to act in ways that promote unity. White brothers and sisters must be careful about having attitudes or using language or terms that are hurtful to their brothers and sisters of color (Romans 14), and black Christians must guard against hard feelings and hostility regarding transgressions of old (cf. 1 Corinthians 13:5). Both black and white brothers and sisters must work to avoid spirits of extremism and ultra-sensitivity. All behavior must be guided by the Golden Rule (Matthew 7:12). Anytime we use the phrase "my people," we should make sure we are speaking of our people in Christ and not those who happen to share our color or ethnicity.

The Bible lights our pathway in life (Psalm 119:105) and answers every false teaching or idea. The book you're now reading was written by four brothers in Christ who believe the Scripture "completely furnishes us to every good work" (2 Timothy 3:16-17) and that it is sufficient to prepare us for answering issues of racial tension. Today the church is made up of congregations whose members are all the same color, and (perhaps more commonly) of congregations composed, more or less, of Christians of diverse colors. People can go to heaven in both of these, but people can't go to heaven while hating or abusing one another (Galatians 5:19-21). The world's solutions are sometimes frightening and divisive, but the Bible is always right. Following Christ means following His last will and Testament rather than the constantly embroiled and changing cultures outside of her.

Wise kitchen-table elders should take people of all colors aside whenever they believe they are saying things or behaving in ways that are unkind to, or in reference to, their fellow Christians of color. They should do this, not because of current political events or out of a desire to be politically correct, but based on what is real and true from the Word and the judgment of those charged by the Holy Spirit to shepherd and rule the church. People erring in behavior toward those of another ethnicity should be corrected by faithful shepherds in clear terms. Faithful elders ought to be in the habit of such corrective meetings with members whenever division is occurring in their church families for whatever reason (Romans 16:17).

Some Christians of color may think that most white Christians harbor some kind of racial animus, whether conscious or unconscious, and may be training their children to believe that white people should generally be viewed with suspicion. Some white Christians may be doing the same regarding black people. Our pulpits and classes must teach how unity works in the church (Ephesians 4:1-3). The church and the New Testament that is her constitution are the answer to racial division among people. Its plea for unity is found in these words: "For you are all sons of God through faith in Christ Jesus. For as many of you as were baptized into Christ have put on Christ. There is neither Jew nor Greek, there is neither slave nor free, there is neither male nor female; for you are all one in Christ Jesus" (Galatians 3:26-28).

Statements such as, "When it comes to racial reconciliation, our churches have a long way to go"[1] is an opinion we do not all share. We know that there are continuing instances of racism and enmity in the hearts of some church members in this country. Yet, from the church's beginning in Acts 2, the Lord's church has consisted of fallible people who strive to serve their King. History tells us that culture often elbows its way into our congregations and historically has done extensive damage. Our goal must be to see all our brothers and sisters through the lens of God's precious will and not through the lens of current culture. The majority of Christians living today, despite their sins (1 John 1:7-9), possess good hearts about Christians who are different from them. We are not perfect, but we unite in serving a Lord who died for people of all nations.

Let's rear our children to love people (especially Christians) of all races equally, to see souls, and to reject the sin that's inside of all cultures. Let's raise them to seek peace and to anticipate heaven with all the people who love the Lord Jesus.

> After these things I looked, and behold, a great multitude which no one could number, of all nations, tribes, peoples, and tongues, standing before the throne and before the Lamb, clothed with white robes, with palm branches in their hands, and crying out with a loud voice, saying, "Salvation belongs to our God who sits on the throne, and to the Lamb!" All the angels stood around the throne and the elders and the four living creatures, and fell on their faces before the throne and worshiped God, saying:
>
> "Amen! Blessing and glory and wisdom,
> Thanksgiving and honor and power and might,
> Be to our God forever and ever.
> Amen."
>
> Then one of the elders answered, saying to me, "Who are these arrayed in white robes, and where did they come

---

1 Barclay Key, "When It Comes to Racial Reconciliation, Our Churches Have a Long Way to Go," *Christian Chronicle*, 1 Mar 2006

from?"

And I said to him, "Sir, you know."

So he said to me, "These are the ones who come out of the great tribulation, and washed their robes and made them white in the blood of the Lamb. Therefore they are before the throne of God, and serve Him day and night in His temple. And He who sits on the throne will dwell among them. They shall neither hunger anymore nor thirst anymore; the sun shall not strike them, nor any heat; for the Lamb who is in the midst of the throne will shepherd them and lead them to living fountains of waters. And God will wipe away every tear from their eyes." (Revelation 7:9-17)

Christians, take heart! Racism is a temporary problem. We serve a Lord who wants unity among His people. True unity can't exist if white people devalue any brothers or sisters in Christ based on skin color or with prejudice. True unity cannot exist if Christians of color extrapolate wrongful words and deeds from American history and assign them to their brothers and sisters in Christ today. One day, faithful people of all nations and ethnicities will be fully united in heaven. Let us live as close to that heavenly state as we can!

We travel each year around the country to visit many congregations of the church of Christ. We seldom see or hear anything that would hint of racism in the church, but we see the opposite over and over. We see people of different races eating together, hugging, talking, laughing, consoling, and serving together as elders and deacons. We see churches that are predominantly white inviting black preachers to hold their meetings or to serve as their located preachers (and vice versa). There is much evidence of love and sincere fellowship from all in these situations.

Christ calls us to put aside our historical angst and become one with people who also have checkered family trees. Galatians 3:27-28 teaches a sweet unity that offers a place where we all recognize that God made us—though we are all unworthy—of one blood. We all put our historic and cultural differences aside and see one another as souls made by and valued by God.

If our culture or subculture disagrees with our Christianity, we must stand for Christianity. There is some evil woven into all cultures from which Christians must distance themselves if they are to go to heaven (Galatians 5:19). There has never been a time when that reality was absent. We must daily test viewpoints we have derived from culture by the standard of the New Testament. Otherwise, our Christianity can be tainted by a feeling that our sinful attitudes are justified. We simultaneously live in two kingdoms—that is America and the church of our King. However, we are not confused about which is the more important. The church is most important. It's the eternal one.

A Christian policeman was asked, "If someone ran a red light and ran in front of another driver, could that driver deliberately hit the offender and still remain legally innocent?" He answered that he could not. The person who ran the light violated the law, but there remains a more dominant law: No driver can *deliberately* cause an accident. So it is the same with the subject in this book—no person can deliberately cause harm to other people. In Christ we live by a higher law.

> But I say to you, love your enemies, bless those who curse you, do good to those who hate you, and pray for those who spitefully use you and persecute you, that you may be sons of your Father in heaven; for He makes His sun rise on the evil and on the good, and sends rain on the just and on the unjust. For if you love those who love you, what reward have you? Do not even the tax collectors do the same? And if you greet your brethren only, what do you do more than others? Do not even the tax collectors do so? Therefore you shall be perfect, just as your Father in heaven is perfect. (Matthew 5:44-48)

When Paul was near execution, he said, "I've fought the good fight" (2 Timothy 4:7). That fight didn't have to do with social issues and worldly politics and inequities—the fight was about standing for Jesus Christ and Him crucified. May it be so with us.

Jesus Christ, His church, and His New Testament is not the problem. The church of Christ is the only solution to racial tensions.

WORKS CITED

Barndt, Joseph R. *Dismantling Racism: The Continuing Challenge to White America*. Minneapolis: Augsburg Books, 1991.

Benner, David G., and Peter C. Hill, eds. *Baker Encyclopedia of Psychology and Counseling*. Grand Rapids: Baker Books, 1999.

Blankenship, Daniel. *Race Relations in the Church of Christ During the Civil Rights Movement*. Muskogee, OK: Breath of Life Press, 2012.

Childress, Clenard, Jr. "The Truth About Margaret Sanger," *BlackGeneocide*, http://www.blackgenocide.org/sanger.html.

Coates, Ta-Nehisi. *We Were Eight Years in Power: An American Tragedy*. New York: One World Publishing, 2017.

Curry, Tommy. "Critical Race Theory," *Encyclopædia Britannica*, https://www.britannica.com/topic/critical-race-theory.

Darwin, Charles. *On the Origin of Species by Means of Natural Selection, Or, the Preservation of Favoured Races in the Struggle for Life*. London: J. Murray, 1859.

-----. *The Descent of Man: And Selection in Relation to Sex*. London: J. Murray, 1871.

Dorman, Jacob S. "Black Israelites aka Black Jews aka Black Hebrews." *Introduction to New and Alternative Religions in America*. Edited by Eugene V. Gallagher and W. Michael Ashcraft. Westport, CT: Greenwood Press, 2006.

Ertelt, Steven. "79% of Planned Parenthood Abortion Clinics Target Blacks, Hispanics," *LifeNews*, https://www.lifenews.com/2012/10/16/79-of-planned-parenthood-abortion-clinics-target-blacks-hispanics/.

Ferguson, Everett. *Backgrounds of Early Christianity*, 2nd ed. Grand Rapids: Eerdmans, 1993.

Hotz, Robert. "Scientists Say Race Has No Biological Basis," *Los Angeles Times*. 20 February 1995. https://www.latimes.com/archives/la-xpm-1995-02-20-mn-34098-story.html.

Jones, Rachel, Lawrence B. Finer, and Susheela Singh. "Characteristics of U.S. Abortion Patients, 2008," *Guttmacher Institute*, https://www.guttmacher.org/report/characteristics-us-abortion-patients-2008.

Kennedy, Duncan. "Antonio Gramsci and the Legal System," 6 *ALSA Forum* 32 (1982).

Key, Barcley. "When It Comes to Racial Reconciliation, Our Churches Have a Long Way to Go," *Christian Chronicle*. 1 March 2016. https://christianchronicle.org/when-it-comes-to-racial-reconciliation-our-churches-have-a-long-way-to-go/.

Lipscomb, David Lipscomb. "Race Prejudice," *Gospel Advocate*, 20 (1878): 120.

Merriam-Webster, Inc. *Merriam-Webster's Collegiate Dictionary*. Springfield, MA: Merriam-Webster, Inc., 2003.

Mullins, Matt. "Is Critical Race Theory 'Unchristian'?" Part 4, *Kingdom Diversity*. 30 May 2019. https://www.sebtskingdomdiversity.com/blog/is-critical-race-theory-unchristian-part-4.

Raffety, William Edward. "Slave, Slavery." Edited by James Orr, John L. Nuelsen, Edgar Y. Mullins, and Morris O. Evans. *The International Standard Bible Encyclopaedia*. Chicago: The Howard-Severance Company, 1915.

Ross, Bobby, Jr. "Delaware Churches — One White, One Black — Find New Life By Merging," *Christian Chronicle*. 25 February 2019. https://christianchronicle.org/delaware-churches-one-white-one-black-find-new-life-by-merging/.

Sanger, Margaret. *What Every Girl Should Know*. New York City: Max N. Maisel, 1916.

Thayer, Joseph Henry. *A Greek-English Lexicon of the New Testament: Being Grimm's Wilke's Clavis Novi Testamenti*. New York: Harper & Brothers., 1889.

Wallace, Foy Esco. "Negro Meetings for White People," *Bible Banner*, March (1941): 7

Wytsma, Ken. *The Myth of Equality: Uncovering the Roots of Injustice and Privilege*. Downers Grove, Illinois: InterVarsity Press, 2017.

SCRIPTURE INDEX

Genesis 1:1 47
Genesis 1:26-27 16, 51, 61, 74
Genesis 5:1-2 74
Genesis 15:2-4 51
Genesis 17:23 49
Genesis 29:21-26 25
Genesis 50:1-3 25

Exodus 2:23-25 49
Exodus 11:1-3 59
Exodus 21:2 49
Exodus 21:5-6 49
Exodus 21:8 50
Exodus 21:26-27 49
Exodus 22:2-3 51
Exodus 23:12 49

Leviticus 5:16 59
Leviticus 19:15 48
Leviticus 25:39 51
Leviticus 25:47-55 50
Leviticus 27:47-55 51

Numbers 5:5-10 59
Numbers 16:22 16
Numbers 27:16 16

Deuteronomy 6:13-14 54
Deuteronomy 7:3-4 64
Deuteronomy 15:12 49

Ruth 1:16 64
Ruth 4:7 25

1 Samuel 16:7 14

2 Kings 4:1 51
2 Kings 5:2ff 51
2 Kings 17:24-41 18

1 Chronicles 2:34-35 51

Ezra 4 19

Job 12:10 16

Psalm 33:6 47
Psalm 82:1-7 48
Psalm 119:105 26, 84
Psalm 119:160 48

Proverbs 16:18 77
Proverbs 18:13 48, 77
Proverbs 20:22 56
Proverbs 23:23 38
Proverbs 24:23 20

Ecclesiastes 12:7 16

Isaiah 8:12 48
Isaiah 42:5 16
Isaiah 57:16 16

Ezekiel 18:20 42

Zechariah 12:1 16

Matthew 5:11-12 35
Matthew 5:24 41
Matthew 5:38-48 56
Matthew 5:44-48 88
Matthew 5:46-47 54
Matthew 6:12, 14-15 39
Matthew 7:12 20, 39, 55, 56, 70, 84
Matthew 7:13-14 21
Matthew 12:50 21
Matthew 16:18 41
Matthew 16:26 16
Matthew 18:15-17 42, 72
Matthew 18:23-25 51
Matthew 22:37-40 63
Matthew 23 54
Matthew 26:28 67
Matthew 28:19-20 81

Luke 7:39 55
Luke 9:23 21

Luke 9:52 19
Luke 10:25-37 18
Luke 10:29-37 19
Luke 17:3 42
Luke 19:1-10 59
Luke 20:25 56
Luke 23:12 22

John 1:1-3 47
John 2:6 25
John 3:1-8 54
John 4:4 19
John 4:7-26 81
John 4:9 19
John 4:24 54
John 4:27 19
John 4:33-34 19
John 4:35 19
John 4:39-42 19
John 7:24 48
John 10:30 61
John 13:34 70
John 13:34-35 46, 61
John 14:6 61
John 17:17 48
John 17:20-21 45, 64

Acts 1:8 20
Acts 2:9-11 26, 67
Acts 5:29 56
Acts 6:1-7 28
Acts 6:2-7 44
Acts 6:3 66
Acts 8:4 67
Acts 8:5 81
Acts 8:12-13 20
Acts 8:26-40 67
Acts 10 32
Acts 10:1-20 81
Acts 10:21-28 81
Acts 10:25-26 54
Acts 10:28 32
Acts 10:34 61
Acts 10:34-35 16, 20, 67, 74

Acts 16:19-21 25
Acts 17:1-9 58
Acts 17:17-28 26
Acts 17:26 13, 22, 74
Acts 17:26-29 23
Acts 19:21-41 58
Acts 20:26-27 37
Acts 22:1-21 76
Acts 23:5-6 76
Acts 25:11 58
Acts 25:13-16 25
Acts 25:17-20 25
Acts 26:1-3 25

Romans 2:11 20
Romans 2:12-16 48
Romans 8:7 22
Romans 8:14 61
Romans 9:30-33 61
Romans 11:33-34 75
Romans 12:2 77, 78
Romans 12:15 76
Romans 12:17-19 56
Romans 12:17-21 48, 57
Romans 12:18 58, 80
Romans 12:20 31
Romans 13:1-7 34, 48, 56
Romans 13:6-8 59
Romans 13:7 53
Romans 14:3-6 53
Romans 14:5 53
Romans 15:25-27 31
Romans 16:17 34, 85

1 Corinthians 1:10 44, 45
1 Corinthians 2:1-2 37
1 Corinthians 4:7 21
1 Corinthians 6:9-11 58
1 Corinthians 6:10 56
1 Corinthians 7:12 65
1 Corinthians 7:20-22 57
1 Corinthians 7:21-23 50
1 Corinthians 7:39 65
1 Corinthians 8:7-13 53
1 Corinthians 9:20-22 26
1 Corinthians 10:31 58
1 Corinthians 11:4-16 25
1 Corinthians 12:12-27 23
1 Corinthians 12:23-25 23
1 Corinthians 13:4-7 71
1 Corinthians 13:5 84
1 Corinthians 13:6 39
1 Corinthians 13:7 39
1 Corinthians 16:14 77

2 Corinthians 5:7 56
2 Corinthians 5:17 43
2 Corinthians 6:14 65
2 Corinthians 9:15 71

Galatians 2:3-5 26
Galatians 2:6-7, 11-15 32
Galatians 2:11 16
Galatians 2:11-14 36, 37, 38
Galatians 2:11-17 81
Galatians 3:26-28 16, 85
Galatians 3:26-29 27, 64, 74
Galatians 3:27-28 3, 44, 87
Galatians 3:27-29 23
Galatians 3:28-29 50
Galatians 4:9-11 54
Galatians 5:13-14 53
Galatians 5:19-21 56, 85
Galatians 5:21 56
Galatians 5:22-23 77
Galatians 5:22-24 71
Galatians 6:1 42
Galatians 6:2 23

Ephesians 2:11-22 15, 61
Ephesians 2:14-16 74, 78
Ephesians 2:15 16
Ephesians 2:19 62
Ephesians 3:1-5 74
Ephesians 3:1-6 46
Ephesians 4:1-3 45, 59, 71, 85
Ephesians 4:4 46
Ephesians 4:23 77
Ephesians 4:26-27 77
Ephesians 5:3 56
Ephesians 5:25 71
Ephesians 6:5-8 50
Ephesians 6:9 20, 50

Philippians 1:27 62
Philippians 2:29 54

Colossians 2:14 32
Colossians 2:16-17 54
Colossians 3:11 50
Colossians 3:12-15 71
Colossians 3:22-24 50
Colossians 4:1 50

1 Thessalonians 5:15 56
1 Thessalonians 5:22 58

1 Timothy 1:9-10 50, 51
1 Timothy 1:9-11 56
1 Timothy 2:1-2 56, 57
1 Timothy 3:1-7 66
1 Timothy 6:1-2 50, 51
1 Timothy 6:4 64

2 Timothy 2:14 64
2 Timothy 2:24-26 67
2 Timothy 3:16-17 26, 48, 70, 84
2 Timothy 4:7 89
2 Timothy 4:8 7

Titus 1:5-9 66
Titus 1:12 17
Titus 1:12-13 55
Titus 2:10 72
Titus 3:1 56

Philemon 34, 50

Hebrews 1:1-2 47
Hebrews 5:14 17
Hebrews 11:31 64
Hebrews 12:9 16
Hebrews 12:14 58

James 1:13-14 69
James 2:1 16, 20, 74
James 2:1-13 64
James 4:4 22
James 4:14 57

1 Peter 1:3-4 24
1 Peter 1:17 20
1 Peter 2:9 34, 56
1 Peter 2:13-17 56
1 Peter 2:18-21 51
1 Peter 2:18-25 50
1 Peter 2:20-23 56
1 Peter 4:8 70
1 Peter 5:6 77

2 Peter 1:5-8 77
2 Peter 3:5 47

1 John 1:7-9 86
1 John 2:15-17 77
1 John 3:15 22
1 John 4:20-21 63

Jude 3 70

Revelation 4:11 54
Revelation 7:9 22
Revelation 7:9-17 87
Revelation 19:10 54
Revelation 22:9 54